Advance Praise for *Gracio*

"This treasure is a must for all that ... intrigued by the shamanic way of living, whether new or experienced. There is nothing I love more in reading a book than to enter into the adventure of a great story and find myself profoundly affected by depth of emotion and experiential wisdom. *Gracious Wild* does this and more in a provocative story that weaves together the raw beauty of nature, the fragility of life, the yearning of the wild, and the sacredness of Spirit through the author's insights, healing, and travels through dimensions and worlds most people know only in their dreams. This exquisitely written book warmly touches hearts and gives flight to the soul, while offering opportunities for healing and cathartic release. Don't be surprised if *Gracious Wild* moves you to tears and helps you experience some spontaneous healing of your own."

—Colleen Deatsman, author of
The Hollow Bone and *Seeing in the Dark*

"*Gracious Wild* illuminates how our animal allies are ever present and persistent teachers, constantly whispering encouragement for us to unfold into the magnificent beings that we humans have the potential to be. With the detail of true 'mouse energy,' Stacey's writing brings the winged-ones to life: seeing the feathers' colors, imagining the breeze created by the flap of a raptor's wing, feeling the presence of the soul of each marvelous bird. A beautifully crafted tale of one woman's journey of awakening to the power of the visible natural world, as well as the unseen, non-ordinary world."

—*E.P.I.C.* magazine–Empowering People,
Inspiring Community

"Stacey Couch's *Gracious Wild* is a fascinating and tender account of her journey into healing, which was aided and mentored by the intimate contact she shared with a series of venerable hawks along the way. A highly recommended, beautifully written story of power and transformation; a lens into a world not often seen or heard from."

—Kay Kamala, editor for
A Journal of Contemporary Shamanism

"Since ancient times, shaman have worked with the spirits of nature, and *Gracious Wild* is an excellent narrative of this work in contemporary society. An intimate and authentic account of one woman's journey from science to shamanism, *Gracious Wild* also offers fascinating insight into the world of hawks and brings inspiration of how everyone can discover grace from the divine spirits of the natural world."

—June Kent, editor for *Indie Shaman* magazine

"Simultaneously realistic and mystical, *Gracious Wild* weaves archetypal themes into the author's personal connection with the proud yet wounded birds of prey who changed her life. Stacey's heart-warming, at times heart-wrenching, narrative scintillates with possibilities the modern human mind normally embraces only in dreams. Reading this soulful, beautifully written book is a shamanic journey into nature's wisdom of renewal, empowerment, compassion, and hope."

—Linda Kohanov, author of *The Tao of Equus*,
Riding between the Worlds, *Way of the Horse*,
and *Power of the Herd*

"*Gracious Wild* is extraordinary in how it shows the profound understanding and soul transformation that can come from inviting the mind to open to the natural world and to connect with it on a deeper level. Stacey Couch beautifully describes her own journey and artfully weaves together her encounters in a way that accesses the draw our souls all feel to nature while also enrapturing our minds in the mystery."

—Christa Mackinnon, psychologist,
psychotherapist, counselor and author of
Shamanism and Spirituality in Therapeutic Practice

"This is a uniquely passionate and powerful book that explores the deepest mysteries of connection within the expressive world of birds. The author's personal journey is so well expressed to enlighten the messages available when we open to this sacred connection. This book will assist readers in transforming their everyday relationships with creation. Inspiring us all to honor, listen, and protect our messengers of the divine."

—Melisa Pearce, author of *Touched by a Horse
Inspirational Deck (Whispers from a Horse's Heart)*

"Our ancient ancestors understood that sacred Nature and her plants, animals, and birds were masterful teacher-healers. *Gracious Wild* is the powerful story of one woman's profound healing in the company of hawks. These birds' timeless wisdom, connection between the Earth and the Sky, and fierce vitality guide the author to embody her soul's truth and step onto the shamanic path. This book is a perfect accompaniment for anyone's healing journey."

—Evelyn C. Rysdyk, author of
Spirit Walking: A Course in Shamanic Power

"In a gripping memoir-narrative, Stacey Couch takes us on an unforgettable and seamless journey from the Dream World to the Real World, from the Scientific World to the Hawk World, from urbanity to wildness. Along the way, we become enthralled by the magic of synchronicity and the joy of spirit mirrors. In the madness of this modern world that we live in, I found *Gracious Wild* to be a gentle oasis of joyous and uplifting sanity."

—Jon Turk, author of *The Raven's Gift:*
A Scientist, a Shaman, and *Their Remarkable*
Journey Through the Siberian Wilderness

Gracious Wild

....

A Shamanic Journey with Hawks

STACEY L.L. COUCH

Antonia —
Enjoy the unfolding
and the journey!

**TURNING
STONE
PRESS**

First published in 2013 by
Turning Stone Press, an imprint of
Red Wheel/Weiser, LLC
With offices at:
665 Third Street, Suite 400
San Francisco, CA 94107
www.redwheelweiser.com

ISBN: 978-1-61852-070-8

Cover design by Jim Warner
Cover image: Stacey L.L. Couch, Peter Schwarz/Shutterstock

Printed in the United States of America
IBT
10 9 8 7 6 5 4 3 2 1

To the lonely and sacred island within us all and the divine spirits that cross open oceans to make our acquaintance there.

Contents

In Gratitude

My appreciation extends to all of the challenging and marvelous mentors and teachers who've crossed my path over the years. Many of you pushed boundaries no one else would and you let nothing stand in the way of your passion. With your help I learned how to release my attachments, embrace my power, and follow my soul's guidance. Thank you.

Thank you to my editor Amber Guetebier for your artful guidance and to Red Wheel/Weiser for giving more authors like me opportunity through your creativity with Turning Stone Press. Many thanks to Sandra Ingerman for both what you've done for the world of modern-day shamanism and for offering the guidance that lead me down the path to my publisher.

Thank you to my mom, Carol Mazur, for teaching me about the light work and power animals, for guiding me to so many brilliant mentors and healers, and for loaning me the best books still in my library. I can't imagine a childhood without *Medicine Cards*, Louise L. Hay, and Clarissa Pinkola Estes. I'm glad you followed your intuition to loan me works by Caroline Myss at exactly the right times.

My heart and soul likely wouldn't have been able to risk what was needed to write this book if it weren't for the love and shelter of my husband's company. Thank you Chris Couch for believing in me, my wild stories, and my unruly heart.

Thank you to Charlotte Rafter for being the wise woman in my life. I count myself lucky to have a mentor as gifted and perceptive as you. David's and your Farm at Dancing Star will always be in my heart. I'd like to extend my gratitude to Juliet Pouillon, Liz Lauth, and Becky Picton. Thanks Juliet and Liz for your insightful and thorough notes on the manuscript.

If only everyone had the chance to have the unfaltering support of a father like Paul Lehmann, the world would be a better place. Thank you, Dad, for sharing in my dreams.

In my heart will always live gratitude for the companionship of my familiars, the felines Gretchen and Inari and the mustangs Cherokee and Legend. The way each of them models loyalty, forgiveness, grace and love is stunning.

At the core of it all are the wild ones . . . the wild ones that are losing their homes, that go unnoticed in our everyday lives, and that have more than we'll ever know to share with us. I plead with you to open your minds, your hearts, and your souls to them. Dare to look into the face of the deer you meet on the trail and see your own reflection. Please release your fears to the wild world and find peace.

Introduction

This story focuses on how Spirit moves through the natural world and the shamanic landscape. Throughout *Gracious Wild*, the reader will find insights into how raptors and other wildlife live, interact with the world, and bring us messages. Fundamental aspects of shamanism are also woven into the story. Herein you will find the essential building blocks of a shamanic practice, such as discovery of shamanic power, experience of shamanic initiation, and acquisition of shamanic training by spirit guides and a mentor shaman. Those of you already involved in shamanic study will find many familiar concepts and possibly some novel ideas as well. In this introduction I aim to give the reader who is unacquainted with shamanism a glimpse into the basic concepts of the field.

What is shamanism?

> Despite its reputation for being ancient or primitive practice, shamanic teachings are as applicable today as they were in ages past. Shamanism continues to be a wellspring of inner wisdom, mystical enlightenment, and healing artistry for all who pursue it.
>
> Matthew Magee,
> *Peruvian Shamanism: The Pachakuti Mesa*

rldview, a spiritual practice, and a
ny researchers have investigated
d the globe and have discovered
me point in the history of every
in *Shamanism: Archaic Techniques*
ael Harner, in *The Way of the Sha-*
piled this information and discussed the
at define shamanism. As a result, they have
ed preserve and develop the understanding of a practice that goes back tens of thousands of years down each
of our ancestral lines.

A shaman is a healer for her community who is
involved in all aspects of health: mental, emotional,
physical, and spiritual. She is the mediator between the
human community and the surrounding environment
(i.e. nature). She performs healing ceremonies to remedy
imbalances, honor that which is greater than us (a.k.a.
"Great Spirit"), and solve mysteries.

Shamanism is the field in which the shaman practices. The uniting themes of shamanism are the journey
trance, a specific journey landscape, a strong bond with
spirit guides, and energetic healing.

What is a journey?

Although she is among the mystics, the shaman stands
alone in her capacity to have ecstatic experiences. These
experiences are referred to as journeys. To enter into the
journey trance, the shaman leaves her body in spirit form
and travels to worlds outside our current reality. A journey is similar to a waking dream where she can ask questions, obtain healings, and interact with spirits.

As Roger Walsh points out in *The World of Shamanism*, the key is that the shaman is trained to both *direct* the journey and *surrender* to it. She consciously leaves her body and travels to other worlds to communicate with spirit guides and then consciously returns to her body, carrying the information and healing. Different than creative visualization, the journey requires that the shaman allow the story to unfold rather than determine the path or outcome. A shaman can enter a journey trace by employing rhythmic percussion, usually in the form of a drum or rattle. The percussion helps quiet the mind and bring the journeyer into alignment with the earth. Some cultures or practices employ psychedelic plants to enter the journey trance, but that is not the technique used in this story.

The shamanic healer gathers information from the other worlds in the form of a story and brings back the story for her client. She assists her client in working with the metaphors in the story and using the guidance therein to inform decisions. Spiritual and energetic healings are also obtained on shamanic journeys, the most common of which are power animal retrieval, extraction, and soul retrieval.

Where are these "other worlds"?

Those who embark on shamanic journeys travel to worlds that are both distant and within. Journeys are just like dreams in that they can come from our own psyche, stem from collective unconscious, or be sent by angels and ancestors. To make sense of the complex and sometimes confusing shamanic experience, a common language is necessary. Shamans use the concept of landscapes as the foundation.

The journey landscape consists of three basic realms: lower, middle, and upper worlds. Middle world is where we humans live, but is outside of time and space. A shaman can cover thousands of miles in a split second in a middle world journey or even go backward or forward in time. Lower world is often associated with the lower chakras of the body, is very earthlike, and is typically more concrete. The shaman accesses lower world by traveling downward through the earth via a central axis such as a tree, cave, or mountain. Upper world is visited by traveling upwards along a central axis and through the heavens. People on shamanic journeys commonly experience flight and can be accompanied by birds when traveling to upper world. It's usually associated with the higher chakras of the body and is often very ethereal, with obscure colors and lights featuring prominently.

What is soul loss?

This can be one of the most puzzling belief systems of shamanic cultures. How can a person lose part or all of their soul? Where does it go?

Soul loss involves, in basic terms, the loss of personal power as a result of a traumatic event or a series of traumatic events. This trauma could be a number of things, from an accident to a physical attack to the loss of a loved one. The part of a person's essence or soul that cannot deal with the trauma splits off and is lost in the unconscious. Soul loss can be as simple as losing our right to voice our opinion to an authority figure or as complex as losing our right to safety in our own home.

Soul loss usually begets soul loss, as the person no longer has the power to protect herself from similarly damaging situations. We often see people who injure the same parts of their bodies over and over or end up in a series of unhealthy relationships. We know this is soul loss when no amount of psychological working or physical therapy heals the wound or prevents the trauma from recurring.

How does soul retrieval work?

The shamanic healer enters into a journey trance to retrieve the part of a client's soul that was lost and brings it back into that person's conscious working. The client then has the ability to choose to live differently.

In her book *Soul Retrieval: Mending the Fragmented Self*, Sandra Ingerman describes how soul retrievals involve finding an image of the lost soul part, speaking with the soul part, and joining it back to the person in this reality. The soul part appears as a reflection of the client at the time the trauma occurred. After talking about the event with the soul part, the shamanic healer asks the soul part if it would like to return. The soul part relays the gift it is bringing back. This is the key healing in this work. The healer is not returning the trauma and associated emotions, but rather the gift, power, and energy that were lost as a result of the event. This is a healing rather than a regression.

This work is not to be taken lightly and must involve a trained professional; the practitioner is dealing with extremely damaging material for the client. The shaman must be clear of agenda, have the client's best interest in focus, and understand how to retrieve the soul part in such a way that the client has access to it. Extensive training and initiation ensure that the shamanic healer is a clear conduit through which spiritual information can flow. Agenda and ego can turn a shaman into a sorcerer. The training and initiation comes from both the practitioner's spirit guides in other worlds and mentors in this world. I strongly urge you choose your shamanic practitioner carefully, to seek recommendations, to investigate a healer's training, and to trust your inner knowing on how best to proceed.

More you need to know.

In this book, conversations with hawks and other wildlife commonly materialize. I do not assume that I know what the birds have to say. The interactions and conversations, body language, outward expressions, and empathy experienced in ordinary reality give insights into the animals' feelings. It is important here to learn how to relate to their worldview without anthropomorphizing. I do that to the best of my ability. In the case of shamanic journeys, enlightenment is gleaned from the metaphors given. The information gathered in these journeys informed the decisions made in regards to the hawks' care and lives. This information is combined with real-world observations, medical expert opinions, advice from dear friends, and that so-neglected gift we all have access to: intuition.

To help the reader assimilate both shamanic and falconry terms, there is a general glossary of terms available in the back of the book.

The names of the people in this book have been changed. Place and organization names are altered or anonymous to honor the autonomy of the organizations that so gracefully offered me the opportunity to learn and grow in my relationship with the wild ones.

I wrote *Gracious Wild* to bring forth the amazing gifts of the animals whose names are here as they were when we stood in the flesh together.

~

PART ONE

Sacred Wild

~

～ 1 ～

Woman Is an Island

I opened my eyes, stretched in my sleeping bag, and looked around. After a few moments, I recognized where I was and realized that I still wasn't. I still wasn't much of anywhere or much of anyone. The dim, rosy light coming in the cracks around the maroon curtains indicated that the sun had broken the horizon but not the thick marine layer. I crawled out of my zipped sleeping bag. Before placing my feet on the cold linoleum floor, I put on thick socks from the base of the twin bunk bed. My watch, easily retrieved off the empty bedside stand, showed that, as usual, I was up five minutes before my alarm. I couldn't stay asleep long enough to escape myself. The cabin was quiet. This meant the wind had died down to a breeze overnight.

I crossed the room in three steps and stood at the open closet. A couple of jackets and a red sweater hung on hangers. The rest of my clothes were piled on the floor in a duffle bag that I never bothered to unpack. I pulled out the same clothes I'd worn the day before and the day before that, and then decided on a fresh thermal shirt. At least I would have the illusion that time was moving. The soft, fresh socks on my feet were a luxury I afforded myself once a day. I went to the window and parted the curtains. The night before I had closed them under the false pretense that a neighbor might see me sleeping. The truth was that twenty-three miles of ocean separated me from civilization. There was no walking out of this loneliness. Another blank, gray day greeted me from outside the window.

The thick walls of the cabin were doing little to keep me warm. Inside it was always cold, even on the sunniest of days. I walked into the kitchen and started a kettle of water on the propane stove. I took a moment to glance out the three windows that faced west. The muted rolling sage and lupine hills spread out below me, and beyond that stood the open ocean. Above was a flat, gray sky. The island appeared in a peaceful mood this morning. I wondered what rapture or torture she had in store for me. My basket of strawberries and carton of yogurt were where I'd left them in the refrigerator. The water in the metal teakettle started to fill the bare cabin with pops and crackles. The slices of strawberries took on the same shape they did yesterday as I sliced them into the same plain white bowl. I carefully shoveled three tablespoons of yogurt over the berries and sprinkled enough granola to cover.

Steam started to escape from the kettle. I turned off the blue flame and poured the boiling water over a fresh tea bag in my floral print mug. The scent of lemon ginger filled the air around me. My muscles, held tense by the cold, softened ever so slightly. I was afforded my first moment of ease in the day. It's amazing what service a hot mug of tea can offer.

I carried my bowl and mug to the bare wooden table. Here I never had to struggle to find my place. The best seat in the house was mine whenever I wanted it. I sat facing the windows.

This was my favorite part of the day. Here I could eat at my own pace while reading the simple landscape through the windows. I liked to pretend that the glass panes were canvas. The view was generally static like a painting, even when the wind howled beyond sixty miles per hour. Then a hawk would fly past or the clouds would dance in shadows on the hills, and I was enraptured. If what I was watching was a painting, it was a magic painting indeed. If what I was viewing was an island, I was hopelessly alone. After I scraped the last strawberry smeared with yogurt from the bowl, I sat, quietly staring, my hands wrapped around the mug. This was likely the warmest I would be all day, and I couldn't help but linger one quiet moment longer.

I planned to venture from my corner of the island into the unknown expanse beyond. I was apprehensive about leaving radio contact, wind-powered electricity, and running water. Either way, I couldn't seem to find my purpose here, so I figured I might as well check and make sure it wasn't over on the other side of the island. According to the map of the three trails on the island, I had a fourteen-mile roundtrip trek ahead of me. I packed a sandwich, lots of snacks, and all the drinking water I would need. After zipping up my windbreaker and strapping on my hip pack, I stopped in the empty office next door to radio in early. It felt good to hear the voice on the other end. The mainland operator wished me a safe hike and reminded me to radio back when I returned. Even though I would carry my radio with me, I would be out of range for the majority of the hike. I didn't pack my cell phone because in the rare times it did work, it only worked near the cabin. If anything were to happen I would have a long wait for help.

I locked up the cabin and office doors and stashed my keys deep in my bag. Just as I closed the curtains every night, I almost always locked the doors when I left. Irrational superstitions lulled me into a tolerable sense of security. The island had a presence as menacing as it was lovely. I often hesitated to turn my back on her.

I drew a shallow breath and set way towards Manzanita Hill. Clouds hugged the horizon all around. There was full daylight now with no warmth of sun. The narrow trail climbed straight up over eight hundred feet, cutting through the knee-high grasses and shrubs. Taller trees and shrubs were conspicuously absent, kept at bay by the constant winds. As I had predicted from my bedroom, the wind from yesterday had not left, but rather died down to a light breeze. Occasionally, the eerie song of a meadowlark traveled to me. The piercing chatter of a song sparrow interrupted the crunch of my footfalls on the loose gravel and dirt.

The sun broke through a small keyhole in the gray clouds as I approached the top of the hill. Blazing rouge rays blasted through and sprinkled pink glitter over the water at the foot of the neighboring island. I wondered if the rosy color was reflected in my cheeks. I smiled at the sun. She didn't show her face much around here, especially this time of year. To avoid the heartbreak of watching her slip back behind the clouds, I hastily turned my back and finished my ascent. The weather station and radio tower waited for me on the hilltop. The anemometer was spinning steadily. These pieces of civilization stood stark against rocks and sparse vegetation.

Then, barely audible, came a lilting foreign chatter. Without any people to listen to, I had memorized the avian voices of the island. Someone speaking a new language had just walked on stage. I followed the music down the trail, keeping my eyes alert for movement, and holding my binoculars. Ahead, a group of robin-sized birds ran zigzags along the ground. Upon closer look through my binoculars, the brown birds displayed surprising yellow and black markings on their faces. The black lines shot up into "horns" on the sides of their heads. Even though I'd never seen these birds before, I guessed from the pictures I'd memorized from my bird book that they were horned larks.

One lark scurried quickly from side to side to check under rocks and vines for a bite to eat. Another paced back and forth like a sentry, anxiously eyeing me. All the while, their sweet voices soothed my empty ears. Then, my alien presence unnerved them enough that they took to the wing and moved from view. I sighed, released my binoculars to hang on my neck, and watched my step as I traveled downhill.

I could see the tallest point on the island, Green Mountain, ahead. The path carried me down into the relatively lush valley between the peaks. A couple of northern harrier hawks incessantly warned each other of my presence as I crossed into their territory. I was frustrated. *Who else could it be?* We all knew I was the only threat around.

Even though the small ravine that cut the valley was dry now, the vegetation on its banks seemed to benefit from the seasonal fresh water source as well as the shelter from wind that the ravine offered. Some bushes even made it to shoulder height here, and most were an intense, deep green that contrasted the sandy, dull green of the sages and lupines. I startled a woodpecker as I wove through the brush. The northern flicker let out an abrupt "Keew!" and made a straight beeline away. There was a sense of normalcy within her red-shafted wings. Here was a creature of city parks and neighborhood woodlots. I was reassured, and carried on with a renewed tempo up the hill.

Green Mountain lived up to its name. It bisected a field of rich, green, knee-high grass that covered the entire leeward side of the mountain. The sun broke free from the clouds again, and I pulled my rosy sunglasses from my pack. A pair of ravens clucked as they flew past me at eye level, wing beats whirring. Their glossy black heads turned to meet my stare. *They must be getting to know me by now.* Every day, many times a day, they would come to check in on my activity. I'd always take the chance to use my voice and say "hello." Now my heart sank as their loud wing beats carried them from view.

I looked westward to the foreign stretch of island below and my stomach clenched. I couldn't point to the source of my anxiety. There were no venomous snakes or spiders, no land predators, no treacherous cliffs to climb, no muggers, no people at all for that matter. I wasn't tempted to go for a swim in the shark-infested waters. As long as I stayed on land, I was in one of the safest places on earth. All I had to do was watch my footing and follow the trail. Like the harrier hawks had reminded me, I was the biggest threat there. The further I walked from my cabin, the deeper I walked into my own company.

The trail flattened out and led me into a dense marsh. Rusty sedges replaced grasses and unfamiliar red-barked shrubs took the place of sage. The soles of my boots were no longer crushing soil. I was buried in dense brush up to my knees, and even though I saw no standing water, my feet were sloshing in my boots. The clouds had returned and the light was flat. My path was nearly impossible to discern. Sometimes I couldn't find where I'd come from or pick out where I was going. All I had to go on was a two-foot-wide trace of stunted foliage. I was sure that if I lost the trail I would lose my mind. There was no escaping this mess. No matter how frantically or carefully I slogged, it seemed to never end.

My feet were freezing. I just wanted to stand and scream. I was so sick of listening to myself complain. I yearned to be rid of the ceaseless mind chatter, but I was afraid if I opened my mouth in exasperation that my wail would never end. I yearned to jump up and down and toss my arms wildly. I worried my tantrum would turn to madness. *Is this what being in my own company is like?* What a nightmare. Now I understood why my life's mission had been to live for my career and find a mate. When I couldn't accomplish those goals, I created drama to fill the space. I didn't know who I was outside this whole operating system of evasion. I was running from my own shadow, and through my fear; my shadow had the upper hand.

This time I couldn't run. I had to solemnly live the nightmare. I relied on a grounding intuition that understood that this marsh, this fear, was only one portion of the island. If I could walk in, I could walk back out. There was no quicksand, no swallowing mud, only my annoying distaste for myself.

The terrain changed. A gently sloping spine of ten-foot hills rose on both sides. Now my path was more defined. I looked up. A pair of piercing eyes stared back from a mysteriously dark, circular face. The hawk stood still, perched atop a bush, the shield of her cinnamon breast in full view. She wore a dark chocolate cape. *Is she a mirage or has she really allowed me to wander so close?* I felt a soft strand of hope spiral between us. The young harrier hawk looked like she had been standing there for centuries, waiting for me to pass. The intimacy of the snug valley was consoling. Then she turned her dark face to something over the crest of the hill, opened her wings, and lifted away. I watched the stark white band at the base of her rump. She coursed from view in a few flaps.

I traversed the remainder of the island in open conversation. The trail moved through numerous identical troughs as deep as ocean liners. I traveled down, then up, a dinghy bobbing in a strong tide. I was well beyond the bounds of civilized behavior, and talked and laughed aloud. It helped to pass the time. In the silence I had too much time to wonder if I'd entered some twist in the cosmic order. *Have time and space folded in on one another?*

I ate lunch at the edge of a rookery of thousands of sea lions and elephant seals. The dozing elephant seals were juxtaposed next to a ridiculous cacophony of sea lions at most a third of their size. Blood in the sand and a soggy, black seal pup indicated a recent birth. Life was raw here.

The mother elephant seals lay with their pups in a checkerboard across the beach. The cows lifted their heads and bickered with long words when another cow broke the three-foot personal space boundary. The sea lions were an entirely different story. Personal space seemed best invaded as they lay in tightly packed herds randomly dispersed along the beach. Whenever someone wanted to go to the other side of the mound they'd just crawl over everyone else.

The water offshore was boiling with commotion. Sea lions in the kelp forest came to the surface, revealing a flipper, nose, or tail. The crashing waves held the most riveting activity. The water was so clear that I could make out the sea lions within the waves. They threw themselves in every direction, some graceful surfers and others rodeo clowns. Their exuberance brought me heartache. This solitary island was a world unto herself, content to carry on with her masterpiece and pass the days as she was. She did not know loneliness. She was alive, complete, and at ease. My soul yearned to know this harmony. For now, I was merely a distant observer.

I couldn't linger much longer than it took to eat my sandwich. I had a long hike back and half a day's work to do when I returned. I turned back to the path, now hauntingly familiar. I talked myself back through the wavy land and soggy marsh, but soon ran out of new topics. The airstream coming off the open ocean had strengthened over the day. My voice and mind grew quiet as I crossed over the tall peaks. The powerful wind over the island stripped whatever thought I could manage from my grasp. I blew back into my cabin late in the afternoon.

My solitary tour on the island was in its fourth of eight days. On the eighth day, the plane would land on the short, dirt runway to take me to the mainland for six days. Then the plane would pick me up at the busy airport amongst screaming freeways and fly me back for eight more lonely days. My life went on in this manner, slow then busy, long then short.

My main responsibility while on the island was to care for a couple dozen foxes in captivity. Due to a chain of ecological tragedies, the endangered fox population on the island was driven nearly to extinction. In an effort to save the genetic line, the foxes were paired and placed in pens with great hope that they would breed. Some pairings had been successful and the population was gradually expanding.

Every day, fog or wind, I made the three-mile round trip to bring them food and water. It took me four to five hours to prepare their food, hike it out, and clean their cages. I was warned to limit my time around the animals so I did not habituate them to people. As a trained biologist, I took this warning seriously and barely ventured to make eye contact with the shy beasts. The foxes rarely stayed out in the open when I was near, especially on windy days.

On the day I made the trek to the other side of the island, I didn't see a single fox at feeding time. After leaving full bowls in every seemingly empty cage, I struggled against the wind to make my way back. The last light of day waned and a quintet of ravens joined me at the far end of the runway. My ears caught wind of a few deep clucks from their throats. I leaned hard, walking into the gale. The giant black birds ceased making headway and hung suspended before me like mobiles strung from the sky. To keep ahead, they were forced to halfway touch down and scamper swiftly along the runway. Then in the dull blue light, they lifted back up and hung. The wind was so loud and the scene so slow that I forgot myself completely.

I was regularly saved from the brink of hopelessness by the tribes of winged ones. I loved the opportunity to watch birds go about their lives without worrying about what impact my presence was having. We were free to interact with one another and could come and go as we pleased.

~

The air was cold and dry on my face. It was weeks later, but it felt like a rebroadcast of the day of that first hike.

The blue skies and sunshine did little to change my mind. Somehow the scene still appeared gray, as if covered by a thin dust. I was returning to my cabin with five-gallon buckets of empty fox food bowls in each hand. Immersed in the drudgery of the task, I stared at the ground, mindless of where I walked. It was a peculiar day, no fog or much wind to speak of, so I had virtually full use of my senses.

An incessant crying off to the east broke my trance. I jerked my eyes up. *I know that voice.* A male northern harrier hawk hovered forty feet in the air. I knew it was a male harrier because of his coat. His back was a pale gray, his underside a stark white, his wingtips jet black, and his rump the characteristic harrier white. He drew a crisp outline against the flat blue sky.

He was behaving erratically, undulating back and forth and up and down across the slope below my cabin. As he turned to change direction, he spiraled and thrust his legs to the sky, sometimes erupting into a barrel roll. At the peak of his flight he rushed into the same chattering cry that had grabbed my awareness. I did not pause to wonder what I was witnessing. All I could do was surrender to the dance. Chills erupted across my skin when a brunette female hawk burst from the ground to join him. They tussled in the air, crying with lungs full of air. This was clearly courting behavior I was privy to. The dashing gray hawk had nearly convinced me to start a nest where he twirled.

For weeks thereafter, I held on to this magic like a child holds onto their imaginary friend. Day after day of fog rolled through. I couldn't understand where all the fog was being created. It seemed as if from some bottomless void. The wind blew steady in excess of fifty miles per hour, carrying a thick marine layer across the island.

Somehow, despite the driving wind, the dense land cloud barely shifted its location. I was lucky to be able to see more than thirty yards most days. Bird song did not carry on the wind. It seemed that whenever the blustery weather did cease, all the avian life took the opportunity to forage and sleep rather than wander or sing. The circular track in my mind became a tunnel. When I grew weary of listening to the repetitive chatter, I released myself to the wind and fog and sat empty in despair. When the depression threatened to swallow me, I fired up a dramatic inner conversation.

Finally, sometime in early March, my world was stamped with the passage of time. *Thank whatever God rules this island.* The wildflowers bloomed. The rolling slopes of lupine below my cabin windows acquired a lovely lavender hue. I was lifted by flaming stalks of red buckwheat, and enchanted by deep fuchsia owl clover faces dotted with yellow and white. Entire hillsides below my cabin were soaked in coreopsis gold. I waded in sunshine.

The coreopsis plant was arguably the most bizarre island inhabitant during any time of the year—a living page in a Dr. Seuss book. Its trunk was about six inches wide, and that had bark layered like dozens of tube socks. The crown of the coreopsis emerged about three to five feet above the ground in a green explosion of fronds. The string-like leaves of the fronds were soft and malleable, like those of a succulent. In the spring, the canopy of each coreopsis would erupt into blooms of dozens of palm-sized yellow flowers. The flowers resembled typical sunflowers, such common décor for an exotic being.

Every morning, I walked into the coreopsis forest to check on the harbor. I followed the trail through the chest-high field of golden blossoms to the crest of the cliff overlooking the bay. There was a large opening in the coreopsis forest here, and an assemblage of large rocks topped by a stone cross stood in the center. This was a monument to a Spanish explorer famous for his exploits in the region. I'd try to get here early while the island was still at rest so I could linger, take in the view of the quiet harbor, and enjoy the short, meditative hike.

Along with the burst into color on the island, I acquired company on my walk to and from the stone cross. Each morning as I crossed the runway and started on the trail, I heard an approaching keen. At first her cry blared, then faded, but as it got closer, it turned into a cease-less yelling. The female harrier hawk appeared, coursing straight at me, her dark eyes piercing mine and her brown wings flapping sharply. She came right at eye level, set on running me down, mouth open, screaming like mad. The trail was gently sloped, bearing me hard upon her. Just as we were about to collide, I abruptly swiveled on my feet to follow the turn of the path downhill. She immediately pivoted on her wingtips to mirror me.

We traveled in tandem, my feet and her wings fall-ing in unison. She hovered just ten or fifteen feet above my left shoulder. At times she'd have more to say and I'd turn to her with some smart quip. *Wonder where I'm going this morning, madam?* Other mornings we'd travel in silence, listening to each other's movement and breath. She became so accustomed to me that I often found her waiting at an old fencepost at the turn in the trail. She'd lift off as I approached and take position at my left flank. Her mate was usually in attendance, but he hung back and watched from afar.

The morning company of the harriers brought me limitless solace. Not only did they offer me much yearned-for companionship, but they sparked a sense of magic in my being that I hadn't remembered. I felt a kind of wonder that brought me out of the scientific detachment I clung to so desperately. With the harriers, I didn't have to pull away and remain swirling in my intellectual dialect. I wasn't required to pose theories and assign numbers to their movement. I was afforded the opportunity to respond and offered the chance to be a part of the experience.

During my enchanting walk each quiet morning, I re-entered a childhood of the natural world. My movement into hawk territory was no guilt-heavy intrusion into a place I didn't belong, but rather a visit home. Here I acquired a sense of awe akin with the wild ones. The maiden harrier's banter was calling me to something bigger than myself, to a purpose I felt stirring in my soul.

⪜ 2 ⪛

The Addled Egg

Spring brought rumors of fox pups. This was why I was here. The endangered animals I was working so hard to care for were going to be around for another generation, but day after day I didn't see any pups. The mothers always heard me coming and were sure to keep the young ones tucked securely away in their dens. I'd put heaping bowls of food in their enclosures, and try not to let my heart hit my toes as I walked away with dirty dishes. This was a time when I couldn't venture to ask myself, *Why am I here?* Even after months of tending to these sweet-faced foxes, they apparently cared little for what I did. I yearned to poke around in a pen or stay and wait for a curious pup to emerge, but I stuck to the rules. I had no audience. I could have done what I pleased, but in the end, it was the meaningless rules that kept me tied to the civilized world. If I gave up the rules, I was admitting that no one was there to catch me in my disobedience. It felt like no one cared what I did just as long as food filled those bowls each afternoon. That sadness was worse than anything. Fortunately, other stories were made available to me.

In April, Eleanor Carroll, a local ornithologist, came out to the island with me to conduct bird surveys. Eleanor needed help visiting a long list of random GPS points on the island. I was elated at the opportunity to work on a project with someone, even if it meant trekking all over the island by myself at the break of dawn. Luckily, my instructions were to only count birds in favorable weather. This meant I had motivation to wander the island, off trail, for hours on quiet, typically sunny mornings. Finally I had sunshine.

On the leeward side of Manzanita Hill, the slight breeze was at a whisper. For once, the sun warmed my bare, cracked hands. I was in between waypoints, traveling due north before heading northeast, watching my feet rather than my surroundings. The red-tailed hawk hovering above and behind me announced her presence by belting out a shattering, harsh call. I jumped forward a few steps and threw my face upward. Then the hair rose on the back of my neck as I met the hawk's stare. We watched each other as she wound a low, tight circle around me as I stood in place. I remembered my uncle and that he loved red-tailed hawks. She headed west on whatever errand called. My uncle was ailing and in the hospital at the time. That evening, my dad called to tell me my uncle had died. His passing was within minutes of the hawk's visit.

For nearly every day outdoors, I had an animal encounter to share. During deep slumber every night, I had at least one vivid, detailed, and completely nonsense dream. However, this was the first time in my life that the creatures of the wild and the visions in my dreams started falling into time and space. The events were related to each other somehow. My uncle came to visit me shortly after his passing.

I was in a huge boat of a green car in the front passenger seat. My fiancé sat behind me, and my uncle was behind the wheel. Before I had any time to wonder where we were going, we pulled into a huge warehouse open on one end to a mature pine forest with an open floor. A wide, dry riverbed passed by and continued off into the woods. We all got out of the car. My uncle invited us on a hike. We agreed to join him. He grabbed a lovely carved wooden walking stick from the car. I'd always known him to need the assistance of a cane to get around. Now the walking stick proved merely a formal accessory. We climbed down from the high cement floor of the warehouse and set foot in the riverbed. Then we began to hike, three abreast.

Another spirit I'd known in this life had been calling on me regularly since I'd come to the island. The woman who was my babysitter when I was a child was like a grandmother to me. She first appeared randomly in my dreams, but then her visits began to take on meaning. I hadn't seen her during the last few years of her life and always regretted never saying goodbye.

I was in a dimly lit living room with the shades drawn. Pauline sat low on an old sofa with green and gold floral print. She was plump like I remembered her in one of her big, soft housedresses. The room was smoky with rays of light coming in through the cracks in the curtains. I knew she was dying.

"You should get going to class," she encouraged. She was right; it was nearly time for my college courses to start.

"I don't want to leave you," I admitted shyly.

"All will be well," she comforted. "Come here and give me a hug."

I approached her and bent over to wrap my arms around the round woman now on in years. She felt frail under my arms. A

*sweet scent filled my senses as her housedress rubbed my chin.
Her tight, gray curls tickled my cheek. Her arms engulfed me. I
leaned into her and whispered, "Goodbye, grandma."*

*I felt myself lifting up with her spirit as it left her body. For
a moment, I held the embrace and reveled in the weightless-
ness. I felt so free. Then, self-conscious, I pulled back into my
own body. I stood aside and watched her spirit ascend.*

My wristwatch alarm woke me from my otherworldly
dream hours before sunrise. I ate breakfast staring at three
black windows and packed carefully for a cross-island
trip. A setting three-quarter moon surrounded by haunting, wispy clouds loomed ahead as I climbed Manzanita
Hill in the dark. The scene was the perfect backdrop for
a horror movie, and after my strange dream it felt as if I
was walking the land of the dead. *What am I doing here?*
In answer, a shrill, blood-curdling scream, erupted from
the darkness around me. I stopped, my muscles surging
in anguish against the fear. I spun to face the tormenting
barn owl. I let out a madwoman's scream of my own. Hearing my voice so similar to his raised my courage. Glowing
in the moonlight, his ghostly white figure stealthily disappeared into the night sky. Just then my grandmother's
house came to mind. *She had owl figures and pictures deco-
rating her entire house.* This was becoming way too real.

～

In the company of scientists I kept my experiences with
ghostly messengers to myself, but I couldn't refrain from
asking about my encounters with the harrier hawks.
On the mainland harriers in low, coursing flight across
marshes and open grassland are a common sight. Before

meeting them on the island I'd mostly viewed them from a vehicle while racing down the highway. My intimate experiences with them out in the middle of the ocean were a personal novelty, but I had a feeling that these unique encounters reached beyond my sphere.

I talked to naturalists and biologists who had been working on the island and its neighbors for years, some in excess of a decade. Not a single person had heard of nesting harriers on my island or any of the neighboring islands. I obtained a copy of the bird surveys for the chain of islands and found no mention of harrier nesting activity. Despite the opportunity for a new scientific discovery, no one else took interest in the harriers until they had a chance to witness the phenomenon for themselves.

Eleanor, the ornithologist, came back most evenings carrying on about pairs of territorial harrier hawks she saw in one place or another. I could say where they met her before she began to speak. We spent one week together on the island and met up for an hour or two each day to recount our experiences. I had nearly as much time alone as usual, but the confirmation of my observations brought a welcome diversion from my doldrums.

Soon, Eleanor was not the only one confirming my suspicions. Jack Asio had been studying deer mice for a number of years and was out for his annual survey. He shared with me that since the decline and now captivity of all the foxes on the island, the deer mouse population had exploded to some of the highest densities ever recorded in all of North America. Each day he set up a huge ten-by-ten grid of live mousetraps and would go back the next morning to check the traps. Each trapped mouse would be weighed, sexed, aged, and ear-tagged before release.

I joined Jack one evening out above Karana Canyon to help set the live traps. Our hike brought us past the coreopsis forest and stone cross, but the female harrier didn't meet us at the trail. I figured she wasn't around because I had company. Jack and I trekked through the canyon and came out on the west side. We worked at specific GPS points for a couple of hours, setting up a grid and pounding stakes into the ground. Then we walked through and set one hundred traps. As we worked, our movements occasionally attracted attention from the male harrier I knew so well. The hawk would circle low, call loudly, and sometimes approach us in a shallow dive. About the time we were finished I couldn't take any more. I looked up at Jack. "So is it time to look for a nest yet?"

He looked back at me with the same gnawing enthusiasm. "Yeah, let's see what we can find."

A smile crossed my face as we left the grid of open mouse traps and began to weave through the brush. I kept my eyes on the male harrier, gauging his intensity in relation to our position. Without realizing, I was testing to see if a game of "hot and cold" would work. The hawk would convey "you're getting warmer" by erupting into steady cries and moving in for a shallow dive over our heads. "You're getting colder" was reflected by a cessation of calling and a distant circling. The harrier was clearly saying "stay away from my nest" while also pointing out where it was. I wondered if by this time the hawk was feeling conflicted. I know I was, because it seemed we were right on top of the dang thing, but we just couldn't find it. I don't know how many times we crossed the same ground. We had searched the area for nearly an hour before I heard Jack's startled voice. I turned on my heels just in time to see the mother harrier launch straight up and out of the brush.

"Here it is!" He yelled the obvious as I was already on my way over. Now we had a furious mama hawk overhead. She had apparently been sitting on that nest just stewing as we wandered around her. Now she was glad for the opportunity to tell us off. We stood with the nest at our toes, staring at the five white eggs in the center. Despite our amazement, we still had to duck to avoid the talons of the mother. The father, by now obviously worn, remained in a supportive role, calling and circling at a distance. The nest was tucked inside a small opening in a stand of lupine and coyotebrush. There was a ring of neatly placed and stamped grasses in which the eggs rested. We took a long look at the surroundings and made a mental note of the location, so we could visit again to monitor the nest. The daylight was waning. "You got it?" Jack asked.

"Yep," I answered as we moved from the nest in tandem and hiked back to the warmth and light of our cabins. My nose wouldn't stop dripping. We were right in the path of the chilling wind off the open ocean. In all of my excitement, I hadn't realized that my fingers were numb. As we made our way through the canyon and past the stone cross towards home, I realized just how close this nest was to my cabin. I could see it from my kitchen windows. Every morning when I sat eating breakfast and sipping hot tea I was watching harrier territory. This explained my frequent sightings of them drifting over the rolling hills of purple lupine and the occasional surprise of a harrier flying within inches of my window.

With the thrill of a new scientific discovery fresh in our hearts, Jack and I went on an exploratory trip to the east end of the island the next afternoon. Both Eleanor and I had run into territorial harriers on separate occasions in the exact same area.

The sun was out and the wind tossed the long yellowing grasslands on the rolling eastern slope. Jack and I crossed the general vicinity where the harrier pair had been seen numerous times, but we did not see any hawks. We then ventured to the north to see if we could relocate a pair of short-eared owls I'd seen during the bird surveys a few weeks earlier. Northern harriers and short-eared owls typically share the same territory and move in relation to prey availability. Jack was very interested to learn if the owls had also recently colonized the island. We didn't spot a single owl. Either the initial sightings had been a passing mirage or the females were tight on the nests and the males were nowhere to be seen. The horrendous wind that whipped across the open plains made the second option likely.

Jack commissioned more of my help each morning in a mouse grid set up northeast of our cabins. In the afternoons, while I was preparing fox meals, Jack ventured out in search of more hawk and owl nesting sites. He had the fortune of sighting a male harrier carry prey into the brush just north of the airstrip and cabins. All he had to do was follow the hawk's trail to find the second nest on the island. It had four downy chicks in it. This was the nest of the courting male harrier I had seen months before.

The morning before the airplane came to take Jack and I back to the mainland, we went to the nests to get GPS coordinates and take photos of the nest habitat and nestlings. Two new chicks had hatched in the first nest. Their down was a pure cream color and it was all they could do to lift their young heads as we approached. Huddled at the edge of the nest, their breath was barely evident from the sides of their bellies. The three eggs of their nestmates sat in the nest bowl, still waiting to expose the life inside. Their mother did all she could to harry us from the nest. We left quickly, with passing glances over our shoulders to see if the mother would land on the nest to warm her young. She remained with us, scolding and chasing until we reached the stone cross. Then she was gone.

The female at the nest below the airstrip was less aggressive, but no less attentive. She kept us in her sights while we hurriedly peeked at the contents of her nest. The four nestlings were older than the newborns we'd just met. They were mobile and did all they could to scramble from the open nest into the surrounding brush. They each found a dense patch of grass and buried their heads, freezing with their cream-colored rumps still in plain view. In the center of the nest laid one perfect egg. We guessed that this egg was addled, given the advanced age of the four nestlings.

∼

In the following weeks, I pored over the scientific literature while contemplating this single egg. I found that northern harriers typically leave unhatched eggs in the nest. Maybe they worked to keep the egg intact to avoid attracting mammalian predators with the scent of fresh yolk. For all I knew, the simple act of carefully working around the addled egg until the young fledged could be in memorial to the life that never came. There was so much potential wrapped in the quiet seamless package. Oddly, I found myself identifying with this one uncracked egg. I felt a strange compassion for the hawk, who would never be handed a meal from her mother's beak or feel the exhilaration of the island wind under her wings.

She'd never be wooed by a sky-dancing male or fight fearlessly for her young. Strangely, I too felt like I was at a standstill. My chance to experience the true joy and real sorrow that these spectacular hawks had the pleasure to navigate was just beyond reach.

As days passed, other scientists came to the island to conduct research in the black-rock tidal pools, ancient archeological sites, rolling grasslands, and prolific seal and sea lion rookeries. I took the occasional opportunity to make short excursions with them and see into their worlds, but I always had to turn back early in the day to the service of hauling food and shoveling poop for a band of foxes that obviously resented my presence. They'd sit in the corner of their pens, glaring at me through slanted eyes. The only time their faces wavered from disdain was when I brought them a whole quail or live mouse. Unfortunately, the mice weren't always easy to trap, and the foxes were only allowed one meal of quail per tour.

Instead of helplessly reaching out to these people and animals that would rather not be bothered, I turned inward in search of the potential I sensed in that silent egg. An eternal ova, I was in a world all my own. I relished the few times a day my head would become quiet and meditative rather than cluttered and chatty. In the mornings, I'd lay in bed recalling my dreams. My recently deceased uncle came back to see me on occasion. The woman who was like a grandmother to me as a child continued to visit me from the afterlife to offer comfort and advice.

She stood before me like the last time I'd seen her. Her green printed housedress was soft with wear. I ran to her, wrapping my arms around her reassuring, round torso. Her big biceps swallowed my tear-strewn face.

"I thought you were dead," I uttered breathlessly, absolutely relieved, and believing every inch of her presence.

"No, my dear," she cooed, *"I've been right here all along."*

The sun cast bright horizontal rays across the island
on a late afternoon in May. I was on my way down to
the closer of the two sets of fox pens. A bucket of full
food bowls was in my hand, opposite the direction of
the island breeze. My eyes were glazed and my head was
turned down toward the descending path. A white body
in mid air pulled me from my slumber.

I blinked my eyes into focus once and then twice, and
a barn owl's pitch black eyes meet mine. In total silence
and seeming slow motion, his round face advanced to
meet mine. When I was sure he would run right into me,
I froze and he gained a foot or so in elevation to skim
over the top of my head. I spun around on my heels and
watched him bank, turn to fly past my shoulder, and turn
again to fly directly at my face.

This was my first encounter with a barn owl in broad
daylight, and I marveled at the size of his head and wing-
span. I understood that he had absolutely no earthly reason to meet me on this path. If he had a nest nearby I
would have seen him here before. If he had been hunting
the mice I was scaring up in the grass, his focus would be
elsewhere. He was intent on me. I remembered my surro-
gate grandmother and smiled in greeting at her messenger.

The encounter with the barn owl was a once in a
lifetime occurrence that lingered with me for days. The
evidence was stacking up. Apparently there was something the spirits, both those on the other side and in the
feather, were trying to communicate to me. I felt like an
idiot because I had no way to translate their messages and

just couldn't understand the obvious. The message had to be simple, but I didn't get it. I knew it had something to do with happiness, because every time I interacted with the birds of prey or had the privilege of an unearthly visitor, I felt something miraculous stir in my soul—true self love.

If a couple pairs of hawks were willing to fly over miles of ocean to make an island their home for the first time in recorded history, they must have had a good reason. I hadn't failed to notice that they also chose to nest within plain view of my cabin. If these hawks were willing to go so far out of their way, the barn owl was willing to interrupt his daily routine, and my family had time to visit my dreams from the afterlife, then I was worth taking note of.

There was a chance that I, in turn, had something to offer them. This was the potential I resonated with in that addled egg. Instead of following researchers I would only know for a week to all ends of the island, I chose to sit in my cabin with a notebook and pen. Who was I? And what did I have to offer? Caroline Myss's book, *Sacred Contracts*, helped me define myself with a simple, yet powerful, set of archetypes: the scientist, the student, the pioneer, the artist, the princess, the healer, the nature child, and the mother. Through these traits, I could map my wounds and my gifts. Without consciously doing so, I was setting my intentions for the healing I needed and the path I wanted my life to take. If my company at the time was any indication, it seemed that my healing and path would be in direct relationship with hawks.

~

Jack Asio and I agreed that it was appropriate to check the hawk nests about once every seven days. In my initial trip to check nests, I found five healthy, downy chicks in the first nest we had discovered together near Karana Canyon. The mother flushed off the nest when I approached and took to fiercely dive bombing me as I stood snapping photos and picking out each of the nestlings. All of the babies were healthy and immaculately clean. My heart swelled with joy to see that each of the lives had come to be. My ecstasy was intensified by adrenaline, which was fueled by the mother hawk I had screaming in my ear.

The female harrier's aggression continued to escalate as her chicks grew. When the chicks began growing in feathers, mama was out for blood. The moment she saw me walk into her territory, she dropped the mouse she held in her talons and came blaring right at me. Her talons came within inches of my scalp and I didn't stop to consider whether she was bluffing or not. I headed straight into the bushes. I knew I looked ridiculous out there, diving to the ground and then standing and waving my hat at a hawk that weighed a fraction of what I did, but I wasn't willing to take any chances.

On my next visit to the nest I wore a hard hat. Primarily, I wanted to get in and out of their territory quickly, which was impossible to do while crawling through the brush. I was also curious to find out if the mother hawk would actually hit me. I could hear the wind rushing through her wings as she barely missed my head. Somehow her screams managed to get even louder with each pass. Then as I began to shut her out and focus my camera lens on the nearly feathered young in the nest, I heard a hard "thunk!" on my hard hat.

"She really hit me!" I said to the young hawks in the nest, a huge grin spreading across my face. They looked back up, mouths agape and wings held out in a defensive posture.

The four harrier nestlings in the nest below the airstrip were a couple weeks older than those in the first nest, so I got to know them best during their awkward adolescent stage. They looked comical and sometimes reptilian with their long pinfeathers and patches of down. Their coats were nothing but rough and uneven. It was hard to believe they'd been those cute, creamy, downy chicks and that soon they would be sleek, graceful fliers. On some visits they would independently shuffle away from me into the grass; on other visits they would freeze and look absolutely helpless. Sometimes I'd find them quietly waiting for Mom or Dad, who were out hunting. Other times, mother was there trying to ward me off. Every time I went to check on this family, I found the addled egg still unharmed in the center of the nest.

Now that the two sets of parents had four or more rapidly growing young to feed, they were more conspicuous than ever. Practically every morning from my kitchen table I would spot at least one harrier coursing over the hills, watching with hawk eyes and listening with owl ears for prey. Often I'd see the couple escorting a red-tailed hawk or raven out of their territory with a bit of roughing up on the way out. I could hear the red-tail's or raven's protest as the harrier's talons grazed its scruff.

On my walk down to the fox pens one afternoon, I saw a male harrier pass a mouse to his mate in mid-air. He dropped it to her from above and she spiraled, talons up, to catch the meal.

About a week later, I visited the nest below the airstrip and carefully collected the addled egg from the nest bowl. It would go to a natural history museum for storage. The egg sat dwarfed in the used chicken egg crate I'd saved for this purpose. The hawk egg was three quarters the size of a chicken egg and still in flawless condition. On my way home, I sat peering out the windows of the plane with the egg resting in my lap. The behemoth blue whales swam below and the meandering coastlines of each island glistened gems of tropical blue and green. This was a stunning day. But my joy slipped away with a sinking feeling. I was as still as the egg resting in my lap, only able to watch it all pass by.

⤝ 3 ⤞

Captive Bred

After years of fieldwork studying everything from gulls and cormorants to yellow-billed cuckoos and willow flycatchers, I had watched the drama of the natural world play out countless times. There is elation when the first chick is spotted just hatched from the egg and sadness when another egg fails to reveal life. The emotions only grow deeper as the young age. There is abysmal remorse at the sight of a starved or diseased chick lying lifeless beside the nest. There is infinite bliss when a fledgling takes her first flight.

To my absolute surprise, in the saga of the harrier families nesting on the island, the addled egg proved to be the lowest point. The nestmates of the unhatched egg were the first to take wing. As I approached their nest in early June, I heard all kinds of crashing in the brush and then saw three of them clumsily launch into the air. I scrambled to snap a photo of one of the fledglings rapidly coursing away from me. They were much darker brown than their mother, which made their white tail bands all the more prominent. I worried the fourth chick hadn't survived and started combing the vegetation around its nest. Tucked away and looking mean as ever stood the fourth chick. He or she was healthy and almost fully feathered. All four of the young harriers were flying on my next visit to their territory.

The parents of the five young hawks from the nest below my kitchen windows worked tirelessly to care for their large brood. During breakfast, I watched them fly over the landscape. Not only did they have to catch enough food for the many mouths, but they also took it upon themselves to keep all potential predators out of their territory. When they weren't hunting, they were chasing a raven or attacking a red-tailed hawk. Luckily, they only had to watch the sky for threats, as all the ground predators on the island were in cages. Over the month of June I had the fortune of seeing each of the five juvenile harriers fly out of their nest.

I knew from my years of schooling and time in the field that fledgling success this high was uncharacteristic. Harrier nests are vulnerable to ground predators, so they choose nesting sites that are in areas of low ground predation pressure. Harriers also select nest sites based on prey availability, and the deer mouse population was booming since predation by wild foxes was absent. In the end, this was a typical scenario in ecology: a niche is left open and another species moves in to fill it, but the story takes on an entirely different meaning in another realm.

When looking into spiritual teachings of various tribal cultures, Jamie Sams and David Carson, authors of *Medicine Cards*, suggest that:

> Contrary fox is as foolish as it is cunning, and
> you may have fooled yourself into believing
> that your low self-esteem is due to your being

born plain or having an ordinary life. This is camouflage of a different sort, in that you have camouflaged your true desire to experience life with friends, with joy, and with purpose. In any case, you are put on notice to be aware of apathy and self-induced boredom. You may have to dig deeply to find what excites you enough to scurry across the wasteland of your dulled senses and *live*.

Like most people on the planet, I had masked my true self with a camouflage made of the drama of familial relationships, obsession with career goals, and worry over monetary gain. Out on the island I had none of these distractions. I was in the wasteland of my dull senses. I was stripped down to the core of who I was and had only the voices in my head to keep me company. Just like the foxes on the island, my camouflage could no longer run wild in my life.

Luckily, I didn't have to seek out what would rouse me out of boredom. Excitement flew to me across the ocean. I found that according to many authors, including Jessica Dawn Palmer, author of *Animal Wisdom*, hawks are symbolically seen as messengers of the gods and are honored for their keen vision. Through my relationship with the harriers, I received the message and the vision of what it is like to actually be a part of the natural world. These moments were fleeting, but brought plenty of incentive to follow that particular vein of being. My almost daily interactions with the hawks convinced me that my life was much more than ordinary. With that realization came an overwhelming sense of responsibility. If I had something out of the ordinary to offer to the world, then I had an obligation to share it. I understood why I and most other people in the world clung greedily to our camouflage. It was daunting to consider the path ahead. I would have to put my heart and soul on the line to find my purpose and live it. If I failed, the results could be catastrophic. My preoccupation with finances and social status were merely surface concerns—I was safe under those pretenses, succeed or fail.

Time after time, I wanted to forget what I was witnessing and slip back into the cozy comatose existence I'd lived my entire life. Then a harrier would cross my path and my spirit would wander with her. Harriers are apart from most hawks we know in that they spend most of their lives actively coursing over the landscape. They do not sit on a perch, patiently waiting for prey to appear. They are out looking and listening for their next meal.

In similar fashion, I walked hundreds of miles during my time on the island without ever actually getting anywhere in particular. Often I wondered what the use of such wandering was until I was caught up in the magnificent simplicity of a blossom by my feet, the dazzling color patterns on a lizard's back, or the haunting song of a meadowlark. These were the meals that nourished my soul.

What was the presence of the harriers telling me about my own evolution? First of all, the contrary camouflage of fox, my social conditioning, had been caged. Second, the medicine of mouse became prolific. As Jaime Sams and David Carson discuss in *Medicine Cards*, mouse energy is about focusing in on the details. It was the magic of details that I thrived on, just as the hawks thrived on the mice. This island was overflowing with tiny miracles. All I had to do was show up and take note.

Around the same time the immature harriers began life on their own, the fox pups began to show their precious faces. First I would just catch a glimpse of their fuzzy bodies scrambling into their dens, the cloud of dust lingering after they were gone, but their natural cat-like curiosity began to get the best of them. They started by sitting motionless in the back of their pens, constantly checking in with Mom and Dad to make sure they were safe. Then, when the young ones realized that I was the one who brought the mouth-watering quail and thrilling live mice, they anticipated my arrival.

The situation escalated as the pups grew, because they took on the fearless sense of immortality characteristic of all adolescents. Their parents became desperate to feed their hungry mouths. Soon I was met at the door by one or more of the members of each family group. I knew the foxes weren't becoming tame because every time I had to wander the pens to clean up their scat they avoided me like the plague. It was simply that the food couldn't come quick enough for the growing babies. Instead of hiding the live mice under a board over the food bowls, I could walk in and toss the mice to the parents by their tails. An all-out soccer match would ensue as the pups chased, caught, and then fought over each mouse. Sometimes I'd see them wrestle just for the sake of play. I couldn't believe the snaps and snarls they doled out. As an only child myself, sibling rivalry was always an enigma.

I was at once sad and overjoyed to watch the pups grow. Sad was the possibility that they could spend their entire lives in captivity and joyous was the knowledge that their unique role in the world would play out for another generation. Admittedly, it was satisfying for me to finally see appreciation in the foxes' faces for the hundreds of hours and miles I put in to care for them. The parents would occasionally look up at me while their pups feasted as if to take in a sigh of relief and say, "thank you." I was humbled and I extended my gratitude for the opportunity to have a window into their lives, but my sense of remorse over being among their captors never subsided. The majority of the fox pairs were without carefree pups, and they went on staring through the walls of their cages in quiet disdain. I was continually ashamed of my species for the selfishness and cowardice that led to environmental disaster and the imminent decline of the foxes. Had the human race not masked their own inner fears with materialism and conquest, the amazing gifts these foxes had to offer the world would not be in peril.

On the day of the year with the most sunlight, I decided to take my last opportunity to wander way off trail in an effort to find one more harrier nest. I'd gotten reports from a botanist of a harassing female harrier down Willow Canyon. It was really windy again, but the sun was shinning steady in honor of the summer solstice. I trampled through the grassland and quickly lost sight of the trail. No matter how many times I hiked away from the trails on the island, I always became uneasy. With that last remnant of civilization out of reach, my mind would play tricks on me.

As I approached the edge of the relatively deep canyon, I spotted a female harrier perched along the gently sloping wall. She saw me at the same instant and took off to the other side. I needed to get in and out of the canyon to follow her. I faced downward; in a troubling optical illusion, it appeared too steep to walk in. I paced along the edge, trying to visualize a safe path down that wouldn't entail sliding on my butt or twisting an ankle. I was frustrated with myself, and it was all I could do to bend my knees and walk down. My logic told me it was safe. My stomach was saying otherwise. I made it to the bottom of the canyon, carefully picking through the bushes and rocks, and then went through the same pacing anguish to choose my path back out the other side.

Once I made it back onto the plateau I was a woman divided. I was too scared to go on yet too stubborn to turn back. Without any external cues that I was in danger, I gave myself no option but to continue. Luckily, the apparition of the maiden harrier reappeared. I focused my binoculars on her swift body tangling with the wind and started walking in her direction. She kept moving away. I kept following. Soon I was trekking up a steep hill; she disappeared from view. *This is foolishness*, I told myself, not sure if I was referring to the wild goose chase I was on or the nearly paralyzing fear I was battling. I stood there for a moment in a foreign landscape, out of sight of all my familiar landmarks and expansive views. I couldn't tell if everything was spinning or if I'd finally become the wind. I decided to give up chasing the hawk.

"I need to accomplish something while I'm out here," I said aloud to myself, recalling an old puzzle I'd never solved. Once I tried to hike to the mouth of Willow Canyon and gave up when I came to a twenty-foot dropoff. Now I could drop into the canyon well below that obstacle and continue downstream to the beach. It sounded simple, but my stomach turned and my back wrenched. I scrambled back to the floor of the ravine and headed towards the ocean. It wasn't long before I felt like I'd stumbled into another world. Everything around me was barren and rocky. There were tall bushes and the occasional sapling. I was totally walled in to a place much more like the deep desert ravines of the American Southwest than islands in the Pacific. The whole experience was too bizarre to handle. I turned and went home the way I had come with no idea how far or near to the beach I'd come.

That day I had the choice to descend to the edge of the ordinary world and become an island unto myself. I had opportunity to leave all my earthly belongings aside and squeeze through the veil into another way of being. All the fear I felt rumbling in my gut and the anxiety bound into my muscles was connected with my inability to reconcile. I had no way of uniting my chance to live the wild way of the wandering harriers with my commitment to love and live in the human world.

∼

Two months later, I stood on a boat in Cathedral Cove and was married to my heart's joy. Close friends and family from all over the country joined us on a magic day full of quiet ocean mist and warming sunshine. Dolphins followed our boat and gulls provided the ceremonial hymn. It was the kind of day written in legend. As long as I live, our wedding day will be among my favorite memories.

I had chosen a fork in the road and that path had no tolerance for lives apart on separate islands. Two months later I turned in my resignation from my position as a fox caretaker when my husband accepted a job out of state. My last encounter with a harrier hawk was on a trail out to the fox pens. I'd given up hope of seeing the harriers much anymore, as the gray weather of autumn was moving in and the call south to warmer climes was surely stirring in their genes. Then, like a parting gift, I spotted a fledgling perched alone among the coyotebrush ahead of me. She was feasting contentedly on a mouse. I paused while she finished her meal and watched her lift off, the wind doing all the labor to fill her wings. That troublesome wind was useful after all. That evening I wrote my final entry in the island log:

The fall bird migration is well underway and we've had yellow-rumped warblers, dark-eyed juncos, Say's phoebes, pacific golden plovers, red-winged blackbirds, and a lone robin visit the island. The flock of willets atop Manzanito Hill was a joy during a rough march to the far side of the island last Wednesday. The fur seals have the most adorable pups with white bellies and masked faces. There were quite a few on the beach over there, and who wouldn't delight in the floppy fur seal flippers? This week has had every day possible on the island. She made sure to show me all of her faces before I left her for good. I got to wake up on a clear calm morning, a foggy windy morning, a windy cloudy morning, and so on. . . . We had visitors from almost all of the places I've ever lived, including the town where I was born. In many ways things have come full circle as this year turns into the winter I arrived in last December.

The foxes continue to carry on their lives as usual. I will miss their little brave, quirky personalities, but I must admit that I will not miss the sadness that overcomes me every time I see their sweet faces criss-crossed by the cage walls. To care for the foxes on this island is to know their imprisonment. The thought came to me early in my career on this island when I was constantly accompanied by ravens. I realized they came to watch me like I went to watch the foxes. The birds were the only truly free creatures on the island because they could come and go to different parts of their life and world as they pleased. As I said . . . to care for the foxes on this island is to know their imprisonment.

I have complete compassion and respect for those who came before, during, and after me. This is not an easy job and the situation is emotionally complicated. It is difficult to work so hard to make these creatures' lives comfortable while knowing and living their loneliness and heartache. I deeply hope that the sacrifice of these foxes' freedom will result in four hundred foxes roaming free to bound, glide, and sprint across the island, their life, and their world. I would like to say thank you to all of the people who work so hard to reach this dream—may you too make it back to your people, your life, and your world, because surely this island is best experienced as a luscious green oasis on the long migration of our lives. So thank you, blessed island, for your insights and intuitions, for your nuances and your guidance, but now it is time that I make my way to my husband's and my future.

❦ 4 ❧

No Trick Pony

It was a mere three months before I came face to face
with a harrier again. This time the circumstances were
drastically different. All winter I had been hiding from
the dreariness and rain of my new environment of the
northwest temperate rainforest. I tried ceaselessly to
find purposeful employment, but instead was left spending my days in a lonely apartment. I desperately needed
somewhere to belong, make friends, and feel of service in
the world. During my hours of Internet searches I came
across a website for a local wildlife rehabilitation center.
I immediately filled out a volunteer form, sent it in, and
called and left a message to let them know how interested
I was. I had an excruciating two-month wait before I was
contacted and invited to a volunteer orientation.

During the orientation, the volunteer coordinator
took us on a tour of the facility. Most of the cages sat
empty and waterlogged.

"Winter is the slow season in wildlife rehab," she
explained to us.

We stopped briefly at each cage that housed an animal and peered in. A porcupine stood still, his back to us.
A red-tailed hawk perched motionless in the large flight

cage. A pair of squirrels raced one lap around their enclosure before disappearing into a box. A sleepy raccoon barely lifted his nose to acknowledge us.

I quietly followed the group, my footsteps contemplatively working the earth there. I did my best to both acknowledge and contain my relief at the chance to do my soul's work again. Other volunteers asked questions now and then. I lingered back, soaking in the peaceful hibernation of the deciduous forest and the quiet babble of the small stream that ran through the property.

We rounded the flight enclosure to return to the clinic and I looked back into the shadows of a small cage. Eyes amidst a dark, circular mask stared back at me. The way the light played on the figures of that face ran chills down my spine. I knew this bird. I paused. Our eyes locked. I dismissed the sensation of a silent, addled egg resting in the palm of my hand. Before I had the chance to give myself permission, I thought: *this is the spirit of the island harrier that never hatched. This is the hawk I never met, the one that never flew free.* The volunteer coordinator, sensing me falling behind the group, turned to say, "Oh yeah, that's Thalia, she's in our birds of prey education program."

I blinked my eyes, shook my head, and turned to face the woman. "Really?"

"Yep, she came in three years ago as a nestling after a haying machine cut over her nest. Her wing was badly broken and she never fully recovered."

I was absolutely stunned. A northern harrier as a falconry bird? The idea had never crossed my mind. It was all I could do to not give myself away entirely. I yearned to hand myself over to this mysterious beast. I longed to have her offer solutions to the questions the island had left unanswered. I wondered if befriending this hawk could help me answer the only question worth posing: "Why can I see the magic of the natural world but not become it?"

It seemed an obvious leap of faith to speculate that a direct-contact relationship with a northern harrier might be the key. The harrier families on the island had already created the window. Now all I needed to know was how to open that window and crawl through. This was all my heart longed to do.

I didn't let on about the monumental implications of my encounter with Thalia. Those in charge at the wildlife center surely would have tossed me out the door on my ass. In fact, I didn't mention her to anyone for weeks. I didn't even venture to peer into her cage again for what seemed like forever. Instead, I threw myself into the satisfying grunt work of wildlife rehab. Cleaning cages, filling food bowls, and learning how to handle everything from owls to woodpeckers became the focus of my week.

Now and then I'd ask questions about volunteering in the education program. I found out that they wanted at least a year, but preferred a two- to three-year commitment from new volunteers. My husband's and my life plans were completely up in the air at that time. I was busy searching out a graduate project to start in the fall, and he was preparing for a field season away from our current home base. Given all indications, we'd be gone for the summer and maybe in Canada by autumn. I dismissed every notion I had about the harrier and worked to stay present in the gifts of each day.

I carefully cataloged my experiences at Willow Brook Wildlife Center and updated my journal with the status of the cases I got to know. I watched an enormous wild turkey recuperate from a gruesome leg wound and had the fortune of releasing a northern flicker (woodpecker) that had recovered from a serious head injury. During the short six weeks of spring I spent at the wildlife center, I assisted in the mending of one red-tailed hawk and watched the decline of another. The porcupine's nervous system condition worsened and he was put down, while the pair of squirrels were released into the woods near the center.

I fell in love with Willow Brook and the sense of home it offered. Then, abruptly, my time there was over. As was the pattern of the last five years of my life, a change in seasons meant a change in places. My husband and I packed up all our belongings and moved across the state to live and work at a wildlife area studying Caspian terns.

As in any wildlife research, we had the chance to witness many beautiful and amazing events over the course of the summer. We watched a bald eagle pair take a green teal on the wing, orange sandhill crane polts wobble through the marsh beside their parents, western grebes run on water in their mating dance, and flocks of thousands of snow geese cloud the sky. We enjoyed the opportunity to finally flesh out our knowledge of waterfowl and to spend our free time exploring the area.

I was available to the wild ones. They had spoken to me so often, but the novelty was finally wearing off. I didn't have a context for it all. The meaning was so lost on me that I sincerely felt I had to abandon the wilderness and try a different way. The empty messages were making me feel the void inside myself more acutely. Privately I dedicated myself to decoding these messages. Publicly I committed to a home life.

The season at the wildlife area would prove to be our last in the field. As always, we thoroughly enjoyed working outdoors together in a remote location, but we were growing weary of the migrant lifestyle of field biologists. We wanted to live in one home for more than six months, get a dog, have a garden, and watch the seasons change. My husband decided to keep his full-time position with benefits through the winter until we figured out where we would eventually "settle." This sent us back to the small town where Willow Brook Wildlife Rehab Center was. We rented a two-bedroom duplex with a big back yard, and my eight-year-old yellow lab came to live with us after spending most of his life with my dad. I was once again without work and went back out to Willow Brook before our boxes were unpacked.

I had returned at the tail end of the summer boom, so there were at least twice as many animals at the center as I'd ever seen. I had the opportunity to bottle feed a fawn for the first time and to help care for a bobcat who had lost her leg to a leg-hold trap. I enjoyed spending a half day at the center and soaked up the experience like a sponge.

Unable to help myself, I started asking questions about Thalia, the northern harrier. I learned that the woman who was her trainer had recently left. The directors of the center were looking to transfer Thalia to a facility where she could get more attention and intensive training. She was difficult to handle, nervous, and reserved. Paradoxically, they weren't sure they could get her transferred until she was more approachable and calm.

Self-conscious and afraid I would seem arrogant, I approached the center's director, Ian Whitham, to see if they needed help preparing Thalia for transfer. He informed me that they had already arranged the move for the hawk and that she would be leaving soon. There was no need for extra help.

Deciding that there was some purpose to me being there, I asked Ian if there was any chance for employment over the winter. "Unfortunately," he told me, "we only hire veterinary technicians in the summer for five months and each position is part time."

I followed my heart down such promising paths and ran into dead ends.

Almost immediately, I was staring a serious depression straight in the eyes. Another winter without work seemed unbearable. I was at a crossroads and much in need of passion in life. Ever since I was a young girl I wanted to be a wildlife biologist. A consummate idealist, I dreamed of saving the planet. After participating in multiple, large conservation projects, I realized that despite appreciating the intellectual pursuit and the time outdoors, I didn't *feel* like I was making a difference. In the moment I was happy, but when I stepped back to look at the big picture, I was discouraged.

My studies were supposed to convince lawmakers and the public to protect species and habitats. My experience was not so idyllic. The research largely served the academic careers of head scientists and aided in procuring funding for more studies. What was the hardest was seeing animals purposefully stressed and, in some instances, lethally sampled to collect data. The studies were promoting conservation of populations and ecosystems, but no matter how hard I tried, I couldn't justify sacrificing the individual for the promise of the whole. I wanted to mend what man had damaged, not cause more harm.

I had chosen the fox caretaking position because I hoped that participation in a captive breeding program would be more fulfilling and compassionate. I wanted to give something back to the wild that had been lost. It made sense—protect and care for an endangered animal so that he and his offspring could run wild again. The reality of seeing a healthy wild animal stuck in a cage for years, possibly the rest of his life, without any stimulation beyond two meals a day was disappointing. The monotony of slugging food day after day for animals that clearly despised their captivity was heartwrenching.

My desire to live my dream of serving wildlife and the planet was lost in disillusionment and doubt, and over and over I became frustrated with my inability to assign a deep meaning to my experiences with the wild ones. I was heartbroken and longing for help. Hopeful that she had a remedy, my mom shared about her experiences with a woman who called herself a shamanic practitioner.

It was then that I secretly recalled a second childhood affinity of mine: medicine women. Even as a very young girl I gravitated to books with stories of intuitive women that healed with herbs. As a twelve-year-old, I relished the time I got to spend with my mother's circle of women practicing lightwork. Since my youth, I had kept a small collection of crystals, loved pulling power animal cards, and had an active dream life. So I was honestly drawn to this experience—grateful to know that what had been a fantasy may now be reality.

~

At the start of my first session with the red-haired shaman Galena Aquila, I met her intensely soft gaze and rambled on about my frustration with the scientific community, my experiences in wild places, and my total lack of purpose. It seemed that any path I went down was a dead end. I had invested my hope in too many broken opportunities and was fearful of the time ahead. Galena decided that it would be best to bring back a symbol to represent my life purpose in addition to conducting a soul retrieval. She explained to me how the shamanic journey was much like a waking dream, which, in light of all my recent dreaming, was believable to me. We discussed soul retrieval as a disconnection from a part of ourselves due to a traumatic experience.

In Galena's studio, we moved from our chairs to lie on a padded rug. I was nearest to her large, lit cabinet full of a rainbow of gemstones. I felt as if I was in the company of old friends. The water in a copper fountain trickled over a round, flat stone. I focused on the babbling sound as Galena started a recording of drums in her headphones. She laid down beside me and fell silent. The room seemed bigger. I could hear the moving water echo off the walls. Then Galena began to speak.

"I'm riding my horse through lower world through a green pasture. Before us is an open, cut wheat field with the sun setting over it. The field is a gorgeous golden color. My horse and I come right to the edge of the field, and my horse stops. The cut wheat is pretty to look at, but apparently impassable. My horse will not go there because it's poky and scratchy. We turn east instead and run along the field's edge. Then we come to the corner of the square field and turn north. Another patch of wheat stubble presents a barrier to us, so we turn east again. We're stair stepping around a series of fields. I look back and notice that we're leaving a path behind us in the tall, soft green grass. This path was not there before. The tall grass is blowing in the wind. We are progressing to the north but mostly going east. I ask my horse, 'Why don't we just go due east?' My horse answers, 'Because north is the place of wisdom and

gratitude. If you don't pass through the north on the medicine wheel you never really own anything. You never really receive, you never really benefit from anything. So we have to get up to the north.'

I'm feeling frustrated and angry that I can't get there from here. I wonder, 'How can we right this medicine?' and ask the owl if he has any suggestions. Owl grabs me by the nape of my neck and flies me over the wheat stubble and to the north. Wheat stubble is manipulated and cultivated by man. Instead of grass to graze and homes for critters, it is a boring wasteland. The fields of wheat stubble appear to go on forever.

Finally, we come to lush, green grass on other side. In the grass there's this round nest, like when an animal beds down. In the nest is a fawn. I curl up with the fawn and become the fawn in the grass. There's such a feeling of contentment and beauty. She grows up really quick and is a beautiful doe that meets a beautiful buck and has a beautiful fawn of her own. It feels like the circle of life. I'm reentering the circle of life. I'm leaving a trail for others to follow. I ask for a symbol for this life purpose. They show me the fawn in the grass circle that is also in the circle of life on the other side of the wheat stubble."

The entire time Galena narrated I saw in my mind's eye the exact landscape she described. It was as if I was there in ordinary reality. The scenery was both breathtaking and hauntingly familiar. Everything made sense. I followed her to a cave where soul parts are often found and watched while she retrieved three soul parts of mine. They appeared as different images of me at the time in my life when I'd been disconnected from them. Then Galena returned to the room with the running fountain, blew the soul parts into my heart and head, and peacefully shook a rattle over my body. She looked me straight in the eye and laid her hand on my shoulder. This was my cue to return my consciousness to the room and sit up with her to discuss what we had seen.

Galena addressed me first. "In the shamanic journey a lot of times the information comes through metaphorically."

She pulled the book *Mary Summer Rain's Guide to Dream Symbols* by Mary Summer Rain and Alex Greystone off her shelf and read. "Wheat signifies some type of nourishment in one's life and usually refers to mental or emotional nourishment."

Galena then continued her post narrative.

"The wheat was already harvested. It was just stubble. To me it seems like it was the educational system that used to nourish you but now it's this barren, hacked off, linear obstacle between you and where you're going. I don't think it's just the educational system, but you'll have to play with it and see what it means to you. We were still moving the right direction, the north, but it was going to take forever. The owl picked me up and carried me over the fields so I had a bridge over it. It's doing it in a different way, rising above it, that is part of the message. It was noteworthy that I was making a path through the grass and then there was a contrail where owl had flown me as well, so I left a trail the whole way. Grass corresponds to spiritual foundations."

She continued. "We were riding connected to the spiritual foundations, the grass, but there is this wheat stubble. The wheat had taken over the land for the grass and we wouldn't go where the barren fields were. I had this feeling like we've been there but we just weren't going there anymore. There was a line in the sand. Then after I was carried over the fields I met a fawn and shapeshifted into the fawn. The fawn becoming a doe that has her own fawn was the whole circle of life. Now you might want to work with deer. Why was it a fawn? What would deer represent?"

Trying to put the building blocks together, I responded. "I just bottle fed a fawn for the first time recently."

Galena pulled the book *Animal Speak* by Ted Andrews from her shelf and read, "Deer . . . gentleness and innocence. A gentle luring to new adventure." She then began to interpret. "You know what hits me with that? You were leaving a trail for others to follow. You're gently luring others to new adventures. That's why you shapeshifted into the deer. The people around you that see the way you live your life will be subtly drawn into a new way of doing things. Does that feel true for you?"

I answered "yes," because in the core of my being I understood everything that had transpired. My mind was light years behind in making sense of the whole thing, but after witnessing a shamanic journey, discussing shape-shifting, and listening to someone talk to spirits, my mind had so much to wrestle with that the voice in my head had grown silent.

I had a beautiful vision for my life's purpose, one that made sense in every cell of my body. It offered me a road map of sorts to my authentic way of being in the world. Needless to say, I was wholeheartedly inspired by the work this woman had done for me. Unfortunately, I had no idea how to apply the romantic tale she'd woven to the ordinary world. How would I use this map of the galaxy to decide which way to travel the small valley I stood in? Could my life purpose symbol help me make day-to-day decisions?

Galena suggested I learn how to journey myself by taking a beginning shamanic journey class. She also offered to continue working with me over the phone since I lived halfway across the country. "I can deliver the soul parts to you long distance."

Before I left I told her of a badly injured squirrel my husband and I had found in a parking lot the day before. It had a major head injury and was seizing when we gathered it into a towel and placed it in a box. We drove across town to a local wildlife rehabilitation center and they euthanized the squirrel because it had a fractured skull. Galena commented, "Oftentimes animals will sacrifice themselves to really get a point across. I get that the message from the suffering squirrel is that you are supposed to be gathering inward during this fall and getting ready for the cave time of winter instead of trying to reach out and find out what you're supposed to be doing. We don't get cave time very often. It's a real blessing when we do."

I tried to cover my frustration with a tone of sarcasm. "I've had a lot of that the last couple of years."

Galena lovingly answered, "This is about coming into your own, to your true work. We can work any job and still do our true work, but we have to come from a place inside of ourselves that aligns with the way life is."

Her words spoke directly at the dilemma I found myself in since my experience on the island. I had seen and understood that the true way life is during months out on the island, but I hadn't learned how to live that way myself. When I returned home from vacation, I found a beginning shamanic journey workshop only forty-five minutes from me the following weekend. It turned out that class was held only once a year. My timing was impeccable.

As I walked down the block searching for the address where the workshop was held, I spotted a squirrel running along the peak of a house. He stopped, sat on his haunches, and looked right at me. I squinted my eyes to read the address on the house and chuckled as I realized the squirrel was standing on the roof under which the workshop was to be held. At this moment I was convinced that I either had an ingenious way of stringing a series of meaningless coincidences together or in the words of Rob Brezsny, author of *Pronoia is the Antidote for Paranoia*, "the whole universe [was] conspiring to shower me with blessings." I soon gave up the notion that I was brilliant enough to write this epic tale and happily surrendered to the gentle shower of miracles.

Like the mouse I met on my first shamanic journey during the workshop, I proceeded to lose myself exploring the details of the things that brought joy to my life. I met and interacted with new animals at Willow Brook, in journey space, and in dreams. This time I could feel a thin strand of connection between what was going on in my ordinary life and the message the animals were offering. Then the link was gone as quickly as it appeared. The inkling of joy I felt during that split second was like the stag leading the hunter further into the night forest. I kept pulling back the shades on cages in the Willow Brook ICU, wondering what message was next. I continued to amble into journey and journal my dreams in the hopes that I'd gather a coherent sentence of enlightenment to bring back.

I had opened the door into my imagination and was constantly being inundated with new stories, landscapes, images, and encounters. I felt both profoundly blessed and overwhelmingly guilty. It was an incredible blessing to be showered with so much spiritual information. What a shame that I couldn't manage to do much of anything with what I was receiving. To help make sense of it all, I had a soul retrieval session with Galena over the phone once a month and completed journey assignments she sent me over email. That line of guidance helped focus my efforts and in turn eased my anxiety. The arduous and slow task ahead was akin to sorting and shelving an enormous library of books. I was starting out with all the books unbound and their pages scattered haphazardly over floor after floor of the building.

That fall I took a part-time minimum wage job delivering flowers for a couple months, and my heart stayed firmly with the animals at Willow Brook. I was there at least a half day a week but typically more. On occasion I would ask about Thalia. The directors at the center had found a facility in Georgia that agreed to take her. There she would receive extensive one-on-one training to become a part of a huge birds of prey show. Sometime in September she was to be driven to a falconer in a neighboring state who would give her some foundational training before sending her on a plane to Georgia. Every time I looked at the white board of cage assignments I would check for Thalia's name, but I never ventured to see her. As fall progressed into winter, her name remained on the board. I asked the education program director, Sandra Cuyler, when Thalia would be leaving. "Thalia has become ill with coccidia and won't be traveling anytime soon." I wondered if Thalia would survive.

The holidays passed and everyone besides me went back to work. A stretch of severe winter weather brought freezing temperatures and a coating of ice on everything, and I spent my caretaking shifts out at Willow Brook alone. Very few volunteers were able to make it to the center because of poor driving conditions.

I stood in the hallway surveying the cage assignments. Almost all of the animals had been brought into the ICU because tree branches were falling on cages and the temperatures were dangerously low. Luckily, we had few patients, so there was plenty of room for everyone. I read the feeding charts and assembled a series of meals. There was a paisley-colored pigeon, a robin, and a screech owl to care for. As I quietly worked in the ICU transferring the birds to clean cages, changing bedding, and washing cage walls, I had three sets of attentive eyes watching. All the education birds were inside. Since they were habituated to people their cages were not covered. The American kestrel falcon, Sped, bobbed his head up and down, watching me work. The great horned owl, Tskili, dozed off from time to time, relatively unconcerned. The northern harrier, Thalia, stood curiously watching me course back and forth across the room. My heart swelled in her company.

The director of the wildlife center burst through the door with a blast of cold air and two boxes in his hands. "Would you mind setting up a cage for each of these pigeons?"

"Sure enough," I replied, opening the cupboards and pulling out towels and bedding. "Have they been fed yet?"

"Nope, they'll need that too," he responded. These two birds were the last of those who'd been outside. Ian would often drop in at the end of the shifts to see how everything was and commission volunteer help. We were developing a working relationship and friendship. He was learning what I was capable of and I was taking in every bit of expertise he had to offer.

Ian had been doing wildlife rehabilitation for decades. From the start I could tell his worldview was somewhat jaded from dealing with the trials of running a non-profit, and he usually came off as overworked. He had a drive and pragmatism about him that betrayed the compassion that compelled him to do this work year after year. I was finding it was easiest to get to know him by working alongside him. He did smile and joke sometimes, but rarely did he open up entirely. That worked for me, as I was in too vulnerable a state to do so myself.

We tended to our individual tasks until I could rally the courage to spark up conversation. "Ian, my husband is looking into going back to school to get his teaching certification, so we are planning on being in the area for the next two years. I was wondering if I could start volunteering in the education program? I'm hoping I can work with Thalia."

Ian was kind and didn't waver in his response. "I'd love to have you in the education program, but we're still planning on transferring Thalia to Georgia once we know she's back to full health. I don't think it would be a good idea for you to start with her for that reason. You should probably start out with one of our more seasoned birds."

"From what I understand Thalia needs to be fit physically, mentally, and emotionally before she can be transferred. I would be willing to commit to her multiple days, if not every day, each week to get her back up to par." I prayed I was not speaking out of turn and hoped my instincts were leading me down the right path.

Ian paused to consider my proposal. "Thalia has never really settled down here. She was raised and trained at a woman's house and was with that woman every day for two or three years. Since she's been here with multiple handlers she's been unmanageable. I do think a consistent handler may make a difference for her. Why don't you talk to Sandra, the education program director, when you get a chance and see what you two can work out?"

Merely an hour later, Sandra walked in the door of the clinic. Ian was still around, so the three of us struck up a conversation and Sandra agreed to start training me in the education program. She also admitted that Thalia could use some extra attention and was open to the possibility of me working with her. Sandra was sure to remind me that I would only be able to work with Thalia if the hawk accepted me and we worked well together. That was exactly the jury I was ready to speak to.

I had a few days before my training started to contemplate my decision to commit to this bird. What if she wouldn't work with me? What if this wasn't the right thing to do? I still had my reservations about holding animals in captivity and wasn't sure I wanted to enter into that ethical and emotional dilemma all over again. Fortunately, Galena had some lovely advice for me. "Journey on this. First ask your power animals if it is in the hawk's best interest to communicate with you at this time. If they say it is, then journey to her and ask if you have her permission to work with her. Then ask her what you need to know and how you can help." I was still in a relative state of disbelief about talking to animals that were incarnate, but Galena's suggestion was the best option I had to find some answers.

In my bedroom with the door closed, I lay down on the floor, placed an eye pillow over my eyes, and pulled a pair of headphones on. The drumming pounded in my ears and I took a deep breath as part of my entrance into the journey trance.

Immediately, a mountain lion, barn owl, and red-tailed hawk joined me. The hawk perched on my right shoulder and ran his beak through my hair. The owl perched on my left hand. I got on my bike and rode down the highway to the wildlife center with the cougar tailing me. I left my bike in the parking lot and walked down through the gates to the cages.

"Is it in Thalia's best interest at this time to communicate with me?" I asked my power animals.

They responded with a resounding, "yes."

At Thalia's cage door, I stopped and asked permission to enter. She gave my winged friends and I permission to enter. The cougar lay patiently waiting outside the door.

"Do I have your permission to work with you?" I questioned.

"You don't need to ask," she answered. This brought me at ease. I had more reason to trust my instincts. The spirit red-tail flew over and landed on the perch beside Thalia.

"What do I need to know and how can I help?" I said, unsure of myself.

"I would like the kind of personalized care and attention that the other education birds receive. Most of the time you and I think alike so you won't have to journey to me to know what to do, but when you're losing your grasp on how to proceed in our relationship, we will need to talk. I can do a lot, like fly far and hunt well, but not enough is expected of me. This frustrates me and causes me to act out."

I was surprised that she had so much to say and posed this question to her. "Why did you get sick then and end up not going to Georgia? It seems to me that you don't want to go there. They would expect a lot of you there. Doesn't this appeal to you?"

"I'm no trick pony," Thalia sharply stated, "I don't want to be around show ponies or be a show pony myself."

The spirit barn owl still perched on my hand turned his head and looked at me. I had a whim of a request for Thalia and decided I had nothing to lose if I asked, "I would love to hear your voice in ordinary reality."

"You miss those harriers on the island, don't you?" she knowingly posed.

The drums sounded the callback beat and it was time for me to return home. "I'll be in to visit you tomorrow," I said before leaving. The red-tailed hawk flew back to my shoulder. I walked through the doorway and got on the cougar's back. He gave me a ride home.

Opening the Door

When I lived on the island I discovered that I was scared of more than I'd ever dreamt of admitting. Even getting up in the morning and placing my feet on the cold floor was frightening, but so was staying in bed half awake, grasping for more oblivious slumber. Once I was conscious of my heartbeat and aware of the sound of the air moving in my lungs, I could not escape. I'd hold my eyes closed for a time, sometimes until my wristwatch beeped its unnecessary alarm, in a desperate attempt to hold my fear in denial. What in the world was I so afraid of? This feeling did not leave me after I left the island. Once I was subject to the fear, I could barely ignore it. Most mornings I yanked myself to my feet, held my breath, and began my day. This tension coursed through my veins like adrenaline in an ensnared rabbit. I was an expert at ignoring what I couldn't explain.

The day I woke to start my training with Thalia I had butterflies in my stomach. As usual, I dismissed the nerves as hunger and got up to treat myself to a sliced orange, a single scrambled egg, and a piece of buttered toast with strawberry jam. I pulled the hot kettle from the stove just before the whistle and poured a cup of tea. As I sat down at our small dinning table, our yellow lab plowed his head into my side. Breakfast time was when he got his first and sometimes best pets of the day. He was always sure to shift his hips under my hands. My fingers dug into the thick fur on his spine. Under my heavy kneading, his lower back slowly released and he grew too weary to stand. He left for one of his three beds and watched me through dozing eyes. I ate contemplatively and glanced out the window at the plum tree in the yard and the street beyond. A dim gray light filtered into the room. Buckwheat started snoring. I sat, my hands cradled around the warm mug, trying to shrug off the damp air.

Annie Douglas met me out at Willow Brook with a smile on her face. She had been a volunteer in the education program there on and off for years, and had been seeing to Thalia's care. As we walked to the back of the property, I was almost immediately happy in Annie's company. She had the casual yet driven style familiar to women who are most comfortable in a pair of hiking boots. She had sunshine in her face, with a few lovely wrinkles brought on by wind. Her blonde-streaked brunette hair was wavy and loose, short enough to pop into a pony tail, long enough to embrace an urge for femininity. Annie was a kindred spirit. She worked in the field studying goshawks every summer. I could hardly believe that she was obviously delighted to share Thalia with me. I was overwhelmingly relieved by her hospitality.

Now it was time to bring the third part of the equation into frame. Annie had me wait around the corner while she went into Thalia's mews (cage—see glossary) to get her on the glove. I waited quietly, trying not to give myself away. Annie's firm whistles and comforting voice wandered from the cage walls. I could tell she was having no luck.

"She doesn't seem too interested today," Annie offered.

I didn't respond, still hoping for the best. I heard Annie sigh and go back to coaxing. Then I barely made out a few flaps of the wing and everything fell silent. Moments later, Annie emerged from the mews, slender hawk on her gloved left hand. Annie invited me to approach. "Did Sandra talk to you about how to walk around a bird on the glove?"

"Yeah, we went over that the other day," I responded, carefully slipping into position in front and to the right of Annie. "Which way are we going?"

"Let's go up to the raptor barn and weigh her first," Annie offered.

I led the way at an easy pace while Annie talked to me about weight management in falconry. She explained that each bird has an optimum working weight. When underweight they are fidgety and too hungry to think. When overweight they can be cranky and unresponsive. She recommended weighing Thalia as often as possible so I could learn more about how she acted in any of the above conditions. Annie talked about how feeling the muscle mass on the keel or breastbone of a bird can also indicate the bird's hunger, but Thalia barely let anyone near her feet, let alone close enough to sneak a finger under her breast feathers. I would have to learn to determine this harrier's meal size based on weight and behavior.

I gave Annie and Thalia a wide berth out of respect for the serene bubble Annie had skillfully placed around them. My back was to them when I felt Thalia pull off the glove and Annie stop. I turned. Thalia had bated (jumped) off the glove in response to the llamas in the neighboring pasture. She flapped and flapped. Annie waited patiently with her arm and hand steady while narrating. "What you want to do when they bate is offer them a fixed point to return to. Never drop your hand or try to follow the bird. Just wait. Thalia almost always makes it back on the glove on her own."

The hawk found her footing and folded her wings. Annie gave her a moment to anchor back onto the glove before continuing forward. Inside, I waited at the end of the hallway in the raptor barn while Annie asked Thalia to step and stand on the scale. Thalia looked like a loaded spring, ready to jump at the slightest noise.

"She has a lot of energy," Annie talked while she read the numbers on the scale. "I think the best thing for her is to fly her regularly. She needs the exercise and is able to fly really well despite her handicap. To get her to fly you'll need to manage her weight closely."

I nodded my head in agreement. I was getting the advice I had hoped for. This meant I was being seriously considered for the position.

We walked back down near Thalia's cage to a long corridor lawn between large flight cages. Annie pulled out a spool of line and attached one end to Thalia's jesses. She showed me that she now had two lines on Thalia, one short and one long. She detached the short leash. By law, permanently handicapped birds of prey aren't allowed free flight. They have a low probability of survival in the wild so there is no reason to risk them running off.

I stepped back as Annie approached the perch and asked Thalia to move onto it. The harrier stepped on to the A-frame perch, busily shifting her long, yellow legs. Annie turned her back and walked a series of paces away, her right hand holding the line attached to the heavy spool on the ground. She stopped, her foot on the line, and ruffled through her hip pouch for a morsel of meat.

Thalia shifted from hyper-focus on Annie to the impending meal on her glove to the canopy surrounding. Annie felt the hawk's uneasiness and moved swiftly. She reached out her left arm with a chunk of quail visible between the fingers of the glove and whistled. Thalia shifted, looked at me, turned back to Annie, and took off, straight for the meat. I was absolutely stunned. On the second flight, Thalia paused longer than she had before, crouching down like she was going to jump, and unfocused on the food. Annie consistently offered the meat with a whistle until Thalia landed on her glove. On the third and fourth flights, Thalia left the perch quicker, but overflew the mark. Annie decided to quit and use the extra pair of hands around to help her clean the harrier's cage.

She "weathered" Thalia out—tethered her to a ground perch—while we took to scrubbing perches and spraying gravel. At one point, we looked out and saw the hawk pulling feathers off the front of her legs. "Ugh, I don't like that she keeps doing this," Annie admitted. "Would you go out and distract her please?"

I was surprised that feather pulling was another problem on the long list for this bird. I stood beside her, moving to catch her attention each time she looked down to pick out another feather. My diversion tactics seemed to work, but it felt like a band-aid on a potentially ugly situation.

During the hour I spent with Annie and the hawk, the gravity of the situation sunk in. What this bird apparently needed more than anything else was an anchor point, some place to ground out her nerves. I could tell after such a short time that Annie was a fabulous falconer. She had more than enough confidence to steady a bird in an unnerving situation. She had quick reflexes and an even hand. She understood raptor body language, read their expressions, and responded appropriately. More importantly, Annie came from a place of true compassion for the winged ones.

Annie was a seasoned pro and I could tell she was frustrated. She did admit that she wished she had more time for Thalia, but I could also tell that she was grasping for answers. If Annie was struggling, the road ahead for Thalia and I was dubious at best.

I decided that I would work my hardest to offer a calm, safe space to this gorgeous beast. It was one of those "if you love enough then everything flows from there" kind of promises. As Annie carried Thalia into her clean cage we all looked up in unison, our eyes drawn to a male northern harrier passing by overhead. I was reminded of the free-flying harrier families I'd known on the island.

A few days later I met with Sandra. She wanted to watch Thalia and me interact to decide if we should continue to work together. By this time Thalia's handlers and Ian had decided not to send the hawk to Georgia for various reasons. So for now, she was at Willow Brook, but I had the sense that if the opportunity arose, she would be transferred. Overwhelmed to have just a few minutes in the company of this marvelous spirit, I did not hesitate to put my heart on the line.

We entered Thalia's mews single file and huddled together by the corner near the door. I worried that two of us in the eight-by-eight-foot cage would make Thalia nervous, but she stood quietly instead. Sandra handed me a white mouse that I held by the tail in my glove between my thumb and palm. I was delighted to see Thalia focus on the food while shuffling along the perch and was even more delighted fifteen seconds later when she came to my glove to devour the mouse. Sandra hurriedly talked me through placing Thalia back on the perch while Thalia was distracted with food, and then we started all over. We repeated this exercise five or six times, with a few glitches. Twice Thalia jumped off my glove before I had her to the perch. She also dropped one of her bits of food by mistake. It seemed my fumbling caused her to trip up, but Sandra had plenty of compassion for the learning process and was pleased with what she'd seen.

My new assignment was to spend time alone with Thalia in her mews a couple days a week so we could become better acquainted. The first day I went in to stand with her for fifteen minutes after I was finished with my animal caretaking shift. This was our initial encounter alone without a cage wall between us. I took a deep breath to quiet the butterflies in my stomach before entering her mews. She reassured me the entire time by sitting quietly on her perch. Up close her demeanor was sweet. My heart lifted to finally see my new friend out of the shadow of anxiety and uncertainty. I wanted to *do* something to touch the moment. It felt fleeting, like an apparition of a harrier on an island coreopsis plant. There were those eyes again, asking me to leave my world and enter into a whole new way of being. I set my intent to learn how to follow her there, and left her to wait for food from one of her four handlers who came later in the day.

That night I dreamt that I was climbing up a tower made of gray stones. This tower looked like it had been built by hand; the outer wall was uneven, with sharp edges sticking out everywhere and gaps in between the rocks. Regardless, there were plenty of good places to sneak my fingers in and get a grasp of the wall as I ascended. The tower sat perched on a house that was perched atop an ocean cliff. When I got to the room at the top of the tower, I crawled through the window. The room was barely big enough to hold me. I started shuffling and pushing against the walls of the room to find a position that was comfortable. The tower began to sway and quake. Then in one graceful slide of rocks, the tower toppled. I emerged from the rubble unscathed and went inside the house on the cliff to talk to the people that lived there. They claimed they'd gone up to the room at the top of the tower numerous times and hung out there for hours. It was clearly my fault that the ancient-looking tower had fallen. I was disappointed that I would have to pay to get it rebuilt.

In looking through *Mary Summer Rain's Guide to Dream Symbols* by Mary Summer Rain and Alex Greystone, I found that "tower exemplifies the super-conscious aspect of the mind where spiritual talents and gifts await to be awakened and utilized." Apparently with all the journey-work and assignments I was doing I had made my way to the top of the tower of my heightened mental awareness. If I had to describe my experiences, this dream offered a fabulous metaphor. The process of learning how to ask useful questions in journey, how to filter out the pertinent information, and how to apply the experience to daily life was much like climbing a rocky tower high above the ocean surf. I was completely exposed and there was no clear path. I was making progress but toward what I was unsure. The feeling of crawling into that small room was one of relief—"Ah, yes, here's what I was looking for"—and restlessness—"I just can't quite get comfortable." I had reached the top of the tower; my mind could make perfect sense of the journey messages. I was writing and discussing the material like it was straight from a college textbook. However, I still felt like I wasn't *really* absorbing the spiritual information.

I had learned throughout my life that I could make my way to goals and paychecks through my intellect. It was a safe place to work and startlingly effective. I didn't have to get wrapped up in the emotions of things or worry that I would go without. With my mind at the helm, I was in charge of my world and could "make" things happen. True enlightenment was the first thing I couldn't make happen with my mind. This was incredibly frightening because it cast doubt across all I was sure I could do. Maybe I never really *did* any of it before. Maybe I wasn't really living. For once, I was willing to admit that all along I hadn't gotten what I wanted. I was only attaining a hopelessly diluted version of my dreams. This was becoming more and more obvious. Now, in my intent to find my way back to the wild ones and live my true dreams, my intellect as I knew it was falling like a handmade tower of stones.

With Thalia, I could make up a well-choreographed story about why we were together, what we needed to accomplish, and how we would get there. I was stringing along a series of serendipitous moments that were logically related, but there was no flesh to the tale, no astounding revelation. In the end, like Thalia, I could not think my way out of the cage. I didn't have access to the key. My true expression was out of reach. Various traumas I'd suffered as a natural consequence of living had caused parts of me to fragment from my conscious self. It was my spiritual damage in the form of soul loss that held me in, just as Thalia's imperfectly healed right wing kept her from coursing over open fields.

I went in to see Thalia around noon. I was able to coax her onto the stump near the front door with a piece of chick. Once her appetite was whetted, she was eager to come to me. The first pounce on my gloved hand was pure bliss. I watched her slender, long legs dance as her fierce talons gripped my fingers hard. She bent down to tear at the meat with her beak. Now I could absorb the scene rather than worry about how it looked to bystanders. I carried her to a perch with fluid steps as she picked the glove clean, asked her to step onto the perch, and returned to my post in the open corner of the mews. We danced, moving and flying from different perches to avoid routine. I wanted every moment, every pounce to be fresh. She chirped a few times in excitement over the tasty activity. It was all I could do to take in her features through the blur of hunger.

Once I finished feeding Thalia the meal I'd prepared, I stood by the door for a while to bask in her presence. She stood quietly on her perch, her crop bulging with food, and set to preening her lovely coat. The mixture of colors in each feather was exposed as she chose one and then another to zip into place. She roused (shook her entire coat) and a shock wave of release coursed through my body.

Instantly aware of herself, she turned her head to look me in the eye. It was as if to say, "Who is this strange woman in my company today?" I felt her legs and wings tense just before she leapt to a perch inches from my shoulder. I held my breath. She released her firm grip on the perch and went back to preening. I exhaled. Her feathers relaxed across the contours of her frame and she cocked her head to meet my gaze. My steady breath was all that broke the silence. The maiden harrier subtly lifted the foot furthest from me while curling it in a loose ball. Her ebony talons disappeared into the thick down on her belly. She was far from the anxious hawk I'd seen pulling feathers from her legs. Likewise, I was miles from the frightened woman trapped on an island. Here stood our window to salvation.

Our next month of training was plagued with paradox. The times I spent alone with Thalia in her mews were serene, heavenly hours. This is where I fell hopelessly in love with this harrier's unbound spirit. She was at once confident, aggressive, and friendly. I worked tenaciously to gain fluidity and strength in my raptor handling skills while she patiently walked me through the process. Even the simple task of accommodating the weight of this one-pound hawk on my outstretched hand could not be taken for granted. My shoulder and arm ached for weeks. I had so much to learn. I could only use five fingers to manipulate her leather ankle jesses through a swivel and onto a leash. It was just like knitting one-handed—the highly tuned muscles in each of my fingers could only remember the motion through repetition. Thalia allowed me to train my right hand over and over. She would often use the time to pick any hint of meat she'd missed off the glove.

The days I met with either Annie or Sandra for training outside the mews varied from hopeful to nerve-wracking. Both women were superior teachers and lovingly supportive. Not for a moment would I ever fault their skills at falconry or at coaching, but regardless of our best efforts Thalia easily slipped into distress. My first attempts to have Thalia step to my glove from a perch outside ended in her flapping wildly at the end of her leash. Sandra was able to work with Thalia and the perch with no incident. Annie diligently walked me through the process on our next outing and Thalia was perfectly calm. Another day, Annie and I had tried everything we could do to get Thalia to step on the scale. To the hawk it was a leg hold trap and there was no way to convince her otherwise. After the struggle over the scale ended, I was able to stand with Thalia resting quietly on my glove while Annie and I talked.

During walks to and from the raptor barn, Thalia would waver from patience to panic. Sometimes the five-minute walk took twenty because we had to stop and wait for her to settle every time she jumped or looked like she would jump. When the wind was unnerving Thalia, Sandra suggested I face her into the wind. For five minutes, this worked fabulously. Thalia roused and was pleased, but then she took back to crouching and holding her wings out—both clear signs of anxiety. Encounters with strange people or dogs also stressed her, but the worst was when we had to grab her, wrap her in a towel, and do health checkups and maintenance. I did my best to hold steady, but the fight or flight response coursing through Thalia's veins automatically raced through mine.

Secretly, I wondered if it was my fear that Thalia was picking up on or vice versa. Regardless, I found very quickly that whatever emotion moved through the hawk also moved through me, often in a physical sensation. Her releasing rouses shook tension from my body. Her panicked body posture froze fear in my muscles. The swings between comfort and fright were severe. Through my experiences with Thalia I was accessing layers of joy and fear I never knew existed in my being. The moments of joy were exhilarating and the flashes of fear were paralyzing. I wasn't sure if Thalia's anxiety was inextricably linked with mine or if it was coming from those around us. I yearned to walk the grounds of Willow Brook alone with her to unwind the mystery.

At the same time I was working out this new relationship, I was still trapped in a struggle to find gainful employment. I had no a sense of direction. Galena suggested I do a journey and ask, "What is my major block to finding my path at this time?"

I journeyed to lower world and met a wolf that led me through the maze of dead-end paths in the dense forest that I had been wandering for years. The paths were worn to dirt from all of my pacing. This time the wolf led me to a grassy path that led out of the dense brush and into an open, old growth coniferous forest. There were no more choices to make along this path—just the squish of soft grass under our feet. Then everything went black and I knew that I was at a point where the landscape was going to be different. First I saw dapples of light and then deciduous trees. Then a whole different forest of shorter trees with an open understory came into focus. It was autumn and the trees were ablaze with red and orange. The wolf disappeared and the fawn, my life purpose animal, was with me. As we talked, I learned that this was a metaphor for where I currently was in my life. I turned around 360 degrees and was surrounded by the colors. The fawn suggested that I paint a picture of what it looked like to me. A blank canvas stood on an easel below an oak tree. It was clear that this place was where all my options were. There was no clear path on the ground. I talked to her about how frightening fall was for me. It was cold, the sun was far away, and the end of the year was near.

"All of these things could bode poorly," I voiced.

"For your future, you have to let go of your fears," she reassured. "There is still plenty to eat this time of year, and the temperatures aren't life-threatening. In the end, winter is not so bad. Most animals find food and enter spring to start anew."

Then an image of a great gray owl swooping down onto an untracked field of snow came into focus. The owl reached out its massive feathered feet, dug them into the snow, pulled out a mouse in her talons, and silently slipped away. I under-stood then that I needed to find a space clear of fear to paint an unbiased picture of where I was and, thus, where I was going.

A few weeks later I had an appointment for a soul retrieval session with Galena over the phone. As the day approached, an experience I'd had in high school continued to haunt me. It seemed the fear I'd tapped into while with Thalia was linked with this memory. I gathered all the courage I could muster as Galena picked up the phone and asked me how I was doing. At first, I answered by sharing my interactions with Thalia and frustration in not being able to quell our shared anxiety. We talked about my experiences a bit and my comfort level increased.

Then I began. "I have something I feel I need to share with you." Even though it had been ten years and I had shared the story to close confidants a number of times, I struggled to proceed. I struggled to give the details of my first sexual encounter with a boy in high school. The experience had been extremely traumatizing for me, despite the fact I was not physically forced. It was worse. In promising me love for sex this boy left me emotionally blackmailed. In pursuing me regardless of my unwavering doubt he left me ruthelessly coerced. In painting me as the culprit he left me hopelessly betrayed. I felt I had made a foolish deal with the devil and lost. The worst part of it all was that he had even turned me against myself. I thought it was my fault.

Galena listened patiently and interjected a question occassionally for clarity's sake until I was nearly through the story, so I was stunned when she came forward with a blunt statement. "I would classify this as rape."

Pausing to gather my bearings, I replied, "I had never allowed myself to call it that because I had no proof to the case, and I didn't fight to stop him."

"But you said 'No.'" I could hear an edge to her voice.

"I did. The problem was that he erased all that when he showed up at school the next day and told everyone that I had seduced him. They all believed him. They all banded together against the school slut, including every one of my friends. He was popular and older and I was new to the school and an outcast, the perfect target. At the time, I took the blame for the incident because I felt I had no choice. I had no external bruises or injuries to prove that I had refused.

To compound the already insurmountable emotional and spiritual pain I'd suffered from the assault itself, I had to take on an abysmal amount of shame. It was a shame I could not justify to anyone. I came into conflict with my parents by requesting to go to another school for reasons I had no way of sharing with them. The loving parents that they were, they eventually accommodated my wishes and transferred me to another school. Ever since I have been trying to move away from this experience."

Galena moved from her center to outright anger. She expressed to me in no uncertain terms that I had been raped. It was in this moment, as I tried to rationalize to her what was not rational, that I saw myself. I saw how terror had frozen me in place and how shame had shut my mouth. I was trying to defend the bastard. After all this time, I was still buying his story more than my own. I could not let the severity of the experience penetrate. I was having a hard time using that label.

Quickly, Galena came back to center—so quickly, in fact, that I nearly forgot how close she'd come to my pain.

She was her trustworthy, loving self again and I felt safe to move to the next stage in our work together. She ventured to do a soul retrieval for me.

The gift she offered me was to go where even I was unwilling. She was guided back to the incident and I was able to observe it from outside myself. While in journey space she accessed and was shown emotions and situations that I hadn't told her about. She even mentioned things I'd forgotten. She explained my experience in words I'd always been too afraid to use. I had the validation I needed to finally counterbalance the exploitation of the incident itself and the months of abuse I suffered at school. Able to view the situation from a balanced, safe place brought on much-needed healing.

Galena brought back two soul parts for me: one lost during the damaging attack and another lost in the halls of the school. With these soul parts came my right to be heard and respected when I said no, to be treated honestly and fairly, and to be able to protect my boundaries without hurting others. I regained my right to have a love that honors who I am returned. The enchantment that made me the seductress and him the champion was broken.

The fallout from this healing was daunting for sure. I got a bad cold within days and released emotions I'd never allowed myself to feel. I had the opportunity to finally process the experience with friends and family and was able to find a sense of wholeness and validation I had lost since the experience. Coming to terms with the concept of "rape" and reframing my experience in that way was both healing and exhausting. My faithful friend offered me comfort where no one else could.

The day after the soul retrieval I got an unexpected call from one of Thalia's handlers. He couldn't make it out to Willow Brook and wondered if I could care for Thalia. I was glad for the opportunity to get out in the fresh air of the cool winter day and spend some time alone with the harrier. Only a few days before, I had gotten permission to take her out for walks on my own, but I hadn't seen her since.

Thalia hadn't eaten the day before because she had bounced around her mews and wouldn't come to the glove for her only male handler. It turns out that he never worked with her again. He was a friendly man with a good heart, but his handling Thalia did not seem to be working for either of them. He commented to me that handling Thalia was like dealing with a traumatized child. He was right.

Thalia's soul was traumatized, and so was mine. In that space we had immense compassion for one another and an ability to empathize with each other like no one else could. That's what brought me to her door and her to my glove.

I could tell she was ravenously hungry from the moment we locked eyes. She crouched down and was ready to pounce on me as I scurried through the door and frantically fumbled through my pouch to get out some food. It seemed if I took too long that I might have a hungry hawk on my shoulder. I got my footing and thrust out my gloved hand. She was on it before the whistle to call her left my lips. She chattered sweetly as she tore at the meat. I carefully reached my bare right hand below my gloved left hand to get ahold of the tips of her jesses and pull them around into the grasp of my glove. Thalia, with her long legs and quick talons, was known to grab people with her feet on occasion, and with how hungry she was today, I wasn't taking any chances. It turned out that she was too preoccupied with the quail to care what I was doing. As I threaded the leather jesses through the swivel and then attached the leash, she busily picked at the glove.

I stood for a moment, drawing in a long deep breath and exhaling out the rush of adrenaline I'd felt as she raced at me for the food. I turned to look at Thalia and her amber eyes met mine. She shuffled on the glove and relaxed her deadly grip on my hand. I felt my fingers tingle as the blood began to flow back into them. I clumsily unlatched the cage door and pulled the curtain to the side. Turning my shoulders parallel to the door, I backed out, watching to be sure Thalia didn't jump off my glove and hit the doorframe. She stood easily perched on my glove. I swung the door shut and closed the latch.

We were outside, free of cage walls and the shadows inside. She leaned down towards the pouch on my hip, spying the quail bits tucked within. Her weight shifted onto my wrist. I tipped my fingers up. She side-shuffled away from my body onto the cradle of my hand. I was learning that hawks always move to higher ground when given the option.

Hastily, I shuttled a piece of meat between my gloved thumb and palm to her graceful beak. She let out more squeaky chatter and, once the meat was gone, took to cleaning those shinny black talons. Like wiping a blade, she zipped each talon through her beak, one by one. This created a magic clicking noise that transported me outside of myself and reminded me of the endless possibility that exists beyond fear, shame, and guilt. One of her inside toes still had a bit of blood on its snakeskin yellow surface. She reached down, ran her beak across the scales, and the red stain was gone.

〜 6 〜

Embracing the Unknown

We identify hawks as predators, whether they're active predators that course over fields in search of mice or passive predators that sit atop snags, watching for rabbits to lazily hop by. The only fear we associate with them is the fear of the prey left struggling in their talons. The human world is inevitably black and white. You're either strong or weak, brave or timid. Many gravitate towards the totem of the hawk in search of courage, cunning, and power. Few stop to think that like any wild animal, the hawk doesn't distinguish between panic and bravery. Thalia moved along this spectrum at any given moment.

Annie Douglas and I spent hours discussing what was the best course of action for the hawk. We wanted nothing but comfort and happiness for the lovely harrier. We tried any number of falconry tricks as well as new methods we dreamed up to calm the hawk. Maybe if she were constantly kept busy she wouldn't have time to notice the swaying branches in the breeze or the passing black dog. Perhaps if we stood still in a motionless room the lack of stimuli would quiet her nerves. Our strategies occasionally worked over the short term.

I was following the same rationale in my own life. Some days I would stay in constant motion, cleaning animal cages, journaling every dream and journey I could muster, fussing over my yellow lab's eating habits, and scouring the newspaper for job openings. Other days I would close the door to my bedroom, pull the blankets over my head, and slip into a blank slumber. No matter what I did, I still found myself bound to a reality, culture, and society that held my senses dull and my joy at bay. I was losing my sense of self, without any hope of living a life full of purpose.

The few options in front of me were weak. I didn't want to enter back into a university system with no promise of employment afterwards. I wasn't interested in moving across the state for another short-term field job. I couldn't bear the thought of working another minimum wage job to make profit for someone who didn't respect me. I loved volunteering but hated not contributing monetarily to my household.

Thalia also had few viable options available to her. Unfit for release, she was inevitably linked to humans. To justify her survival she had to be of service, some use in the human world. There were two options for her. The track she'd been on the majority of her life involved being an ambassador bird. This meant she was to attend twelve raptor education presentations a year. Willow Brook was invited to a variety of venues, including classrooms, Boy Scout meetings, retirement homes, and community fairs. As an ambassador bird, Thalia would have to remain calm in any of these environments.

The second option for her was to be a display bird. In this service, the harrier would have to sit quietly in her mews while a host of glaring eyes penetrated the depths of her cage. Like the animals in a zoo, she would have little personal space of her own. As a display bird, she would likely miss the opportunity to go outside her cage for walks or flights on a tether. I knew that her boundless energy would go untapped and instead erupt within the confines of her cage walls, especially with the invasion of onlooking eyes. Others in the education program had the same sense about Thalia. To remain in this world, she had to perform well in front of a crowd.

It had been a couple of months since Thalia had fallen ill. To avoid recontamination, we had kept Thalia out of her usual mews until the elements had time to break down any disease left lurking in the gravel and perches. Annie and I talked and realized that we could move Thalia back into the mews inside the raptor barn adjacent to the clinic. Annie had fond memories of working with Thalia in the room of the raptor barn, and we were hopeful that Thalia would find solace in her old home.

It was hard to tell if she was more comfortable. When I'd look in at her sitting on the ten-foot-high perch along the wall, she seemed more settled than I'd seen her. Some days she'd meet us at the door and come straight to our gloves. Other days we couldn't coax her within five feet of us. In my mind, I was seeing progress, but Thalia still wasn't as consistent as Willow Brook needed for her to be an ambassador bird. I needed to be able to get her on the glove on any given day, especially on days when presentations were scheduled. Then I needed to be able to trust that she would handle most, if not all, audiences calmly. I decided that if I needed consistency from her then I needed to offer her the same. Annie and I worked hard over the next month to match our routines and share creative solutions.

One afternoon in warm spring weather, I met Annie out at Willow Brook. This was to be our last day together with Thalia because Annie was leaving to do field research for the summer. I had asked her to meet with me not only because I wanted a chance to say goodbye, but also because I wanted hands-on instruction on how to fly Thalia.

I walked with Annie as she carried Thalia down the road to the corridor lawn and A-frame perch. She walked me through the procedure for hooking the flying line up to Thalia's jesses and narrated as she called Thalia to her glove a handful of times. Thalia was focused and obedient, hitting the mark every time. I watched and listened, diligently trying to pick up every nuance of Annie's methods. I'd seen this all before, but would now have to put it to use.

Annie set the brunette hawk on the perch and walked over to hand me the pouch of food and flying line. I made sure to get everything set up as I needed it. We watched the harrier out of the corner of our eyes to make sure she was still. Thalia sat nonchalantly, facing straight ahead.

I walked in an arch to a point twenty to twenty-five feet away and turned my back to the bird. I kept my hands in front of me and out of her view while stuffing a large chunk of meat into my gloved hand. I double-checked the line to make sure it was firmly under my left foot. Both of my feet were firmly planted in the grass, shoulder width apart. There was little room for doubt here. Thalia wouldn't think of flying towards a shred of fear. I took a breath in and let it out, feeling my energy sink into the ground. *If I'm going to be a raptor perch, I need to stand rooted like a tree*, I thought to myself. I raised my left hand out parallel to the ground, held steady, looked over my left shoulder, and whistled.

Thalia crouched, her body tense but lithe. Every feather on her body lay smooth in the instant before her wings extended and legs pushed off. Now she was five times the size I'd ever seen her before. I stood from the perspective of a mouse, surprised to a standstill. Her wings drew in and out with my breath. One beat and a quick glide. Two beats and I could feel her stare penetrate my soul. Stretched across my entire line of vision was this fabulous creature. Just as I was sure she was coming straight at my head, she rotated a fingertip. The sound of her feet hitting the leather of my glove was deafening. The clutch she had on my hand was crushing. I reminded my lungs to draw in air while the huntress devoured her prey.

This was a split in the canvas where the world around was no more and I stood with both feet in another. Here was the infinite spirit I knew lived within this crippled body. Through this vision she'd offered me a direct link to the vastness beyond the mundane. A sense of hope, which I hadn't felt since I couldn't remember how long, welled into the beaming smile on my face. I now held in my heart a true vision of my own soul along with that of my dear friend. She had leapt over that last gap between my true promptings and myself. What a miraculous gift. I carefully slipped back through the veil and turned to face Annie. She was smiling.

I repeated this profound exercise a handful more times until Thalia and I both lost our focus. It was exhausting to hold such sacredness amidst the weight of the reality we were bound to. She flew past my glove and landed in the grass beyond.

"Let's call it," Annie interrupted, "and end on a good note." She turned and went into the kestrel falcon's mews to get him on the glove for a visit while I switched Thalia's leashes. In the kestrel's charming, sassy way, he twitched and danced contentedly on Annie's glove. His small stature and bold attitude brought a much-needed buoyancy to the air. The four of us stood in the mid-morning sunshine, enjoying casual conversation. Thalia and I stood with our backs to the sun, digesting the experience.

Then Thalia did something we had never seen her do before. She made careful adjustments to position her shoulders perfectly perpendicular to the sun's rays. Like a vulture warming its black coat, she arched her wings to catch the heat and bowed her gorgeous head in praise. We stood speechless, afraid to unsettle the well-crafted sculpture that stood on my glove. She was astounding in her confidence, glaring in her truth.

Days after Annie left town, I slipped and sprained my ankle. This meant I didn't get to see Thalia for a handful of days, and she had a different person showing up every day to feed her. For a week afterwards, we went on slow, bumpy walks together as I nursed myself back to health. The irony was not lost on me. Our footing was assuredly unsound. Each day I walked into her mews I was never sure what her response would be. She ranged from complete disinterest to mild curiosity to downright enthusiasm. I weighed her and her food every time I worked with her to try and manage her behavior. Just when I thought I had a working formula, she would have nothing to do with me. I cared for her seven days a week. I tried to work with her at the exact same time every day, wondering if a variation of a couple hours was the trouble. When she lapsed into even thirty seconds of feather-pulling in her crate or mews, all our triumphs were erased. When, after fifteen to twenty minutes of coaxing, she still insisted on ignoring my pleas to take her out, I was devastated. It was soul-wrenching work.

I was afforded the occasional fortune of getting to fly her in the open air. The number of times she'd come to my glove were limited, so I relished every moment I got to look over my shoulder and see her owl-like face and intense hawk stare coming straight for me. These moments were what gave me the hope I needed during the empty time I was left with when I couldn't get her out.

Annie, Sandra, and I had discussed the long list of possible causes of Thalia's inconsistency. Annie knew that Thalia had a cataract in her right eye, the one closest to us when we had her on the glove. In Annie's opinion, the cataract had grown over the past few months and likely caused a significant blind spot. I sided with her and understood that such a handicap could be unnerving. Thalia could be missing a profound amount of her handlers' body language and cues. I made an appointment with a local veterinarian who was an eye specialist.

On the day I was scheduled to take Thalia in, I decided to spend some time alone with her outside the confines of the wildlife center proper and the worry associated with her place there. If her prognosis was bad, we would have to put her into retirement, a life forever behind walls. I was able to get her to my glove by making a trail of food bits on perches that led to me. She was jumpy around the scale, but during our walk to the back of Willow Brook's property her mood was more agreeable.

Once we got to the marshy, small field at the back of the property I relaxed in the open, sunny air. It felt good to be away from the complex of cages and pens, out from underneath the dense canopy, and in our own private world. Thalia settled down fairly quickly too. She set to scanning the high and low spots of the marsh, seeking out wandering mice or fluttering songbirds. Then it hit me—this was the kind of habitat she would have lived in.

Unencumbered by the potential intrusion of human ears, I became comfortable enough to talk aloud to the hawk. I hadn't talked to a harrier like this since living on the island. I spoke an imaginary tale of the life she should have had as a marsh hawk. The path was so tangible in that moment. I felt her spirit coursing through the tall grass, flashing in the sunlight. But there she stood on my glove, beautiful, with the intensely blue sky and small fluffy clouds behind her regal head. She was stunning as she stood on my hand, tethered to human whims. It was then that I apologized profusely, with tears streaming down my face for the dampening life that she was left with. She turned and looked at me with a slight twist of her head. These were likely the first tears she'd ever witnessed, and she obviously recognized their importance. As I looked out at the field through blurry eyes, a hummingbird came into view. He was hovering at a safe distance, looking right at us. I recognized the little hummer as a sacred love charm cementing our bond outside of time and space. All I heard were his wings and the water slowly trickling through the reeds. All I felt was the largely unexplored connection between the hawk and I. In that moment, I knew that if I were a bird, I would be Thalia. I saw more of myself when I looked at her than I did when looking in a mirror. To me I was she.

My relationship with the maiden harrier caused me to struggle immensely with the dominance paradigm of falconry. Why was it that Thalia was locked in servitude to humans? How could you measure the value of a life in such a way? I held no resentment towards the people who ran the wildlife center, but rather the crumby system we all were operating in. Ultimately this struggle embodied my crisis over the confines of human civilization. My life too was valueless if I wasn't out making money, being a servicing component of the technological wheel. I had chosen a career in wildlife biology in an attempt to step outside the societal constraints I saw eating up my family and everyone around me. What I had learned in the process was that it's extremely difficult to live on the fringe of society and still have a home, family, and creature comforts. That wasn't the life for me either, so what was?

The vet confirmed that Thalia had a cataract in her right eye, but she couldn't tell me how much it was impairing her vision. The vet asked me, "Is she landing on perches okay?"

"Well, yes," I answered, trying not to sound defensive, "but her cage isn't that big and the perches are always in the same place." *For heaven's sake*, I thought to myself, *I know the way around my own house with one eye closed.*

"I don't think it's her vision then that's causing her behavioral problems. My suggestion is to put her in a different cage," the vet responded in a condescending voice.

The fury in my chest quickly rose and I did everything I could not to show it. I knew that Thalia was in the best possible living situation I could offer her. She was working better for me there than in the other cages we'd had her in. Annie had the same experience. I knew Thalia's cage was not the problem because we'd tried a handful of environments, and a switch might actually make things worse. I was frustrated that a vet who treated eye problems in common pets was giving me advice on raptor behavior, but felt no recourse to argue. I was left to solve the problem on my own.

It did not escape me that Thalia's cataract provided apt metaphor for my current situation. I was operating partially blind, forced to make decisions without a huge chunk of the picture. In one day I had to decide between a windfall of job offers. One promised good pay, status, and security working as a full time manager at a shoe repair shop. Another offered the opportunity to be outdoors and learn about gardening at a nursery full time. A third offered weekend employment for little pay and was a considerable drive from my house at a lovely organic farm. All I could do was follow my heart's desire and trust.

Within a week of our visit to the vet, I began the job at the local organic farm. I worked weekends in their store selling fresh produce and baked goods and serving lunches. I'd taken the job not because I'd always dreamed of being a waitress, but because the moment I drove into the parking lot beside the huge barn I felt at home. When I walked into the farmstand to meet the owners I knew that was where I needed to be.

Between my weekend job at the farm and the part-time position I hoped to get as a veterinary technician at Willow Brook, I would have a decent income and a busy summer. Everything wasn't clicking together at once or in any rational order, so I had to take each piece as it came and trust that my vision would come together in time. I was learning how to view with my heart and entrust my path in the hands of Spirit. This was in stark contrast to the intense "make it happen" attitude of American culture.

The whole picture of Thalia's future was also slowly piecing together, but it was much less encouraging. Most days I wasn't willing to look at the obvious. Given the constraints on her life, she wasn't happy to live it anymore. There was no medical treatment for her condition, no option available we hadn't tried. Her body was creating a blind spot in her vision, so she wouldn't have to see the life she was bound to. Regardless, I kept trying to hold in place our progress together against a rising wave of defeats. By late spring, we had gone to two presentations. She'd done fairly well at each, quietly standing on my glove for fifteen to twenty minutes in front of the crowd before releasing her adrenaline in a series of bates and panting. When she would get nervous I'd shuttle her back into her travel crate and away from piercing eyes. I figured she could only get better with practice, so I signed us up for a third presentation.

The presentation was at a private elementary school across town for a couple of second grade classes. We drove there in the middle of the day in Willow Brook's pickup truck. The heat of summer was starting to set in, so we left the windows on the pickup canopy open. The presentation was scheduled to be in a lobby on the second floor of the school. We had to load the birds' travel crates onto a cart and wheel the cart into and out of an elevator. The kids could barely contain themselves as they filed in to sit on the floor. They were all wiggles and squirms. We couldn't help but smile.

As we waited for all of them to get situated, I lifted the blanket covering Thalia's travel crate and peeked in. She glared back, absolutely panicked, with a pile of down feathers around her. My heart shattered. I had to quietly release the blanket, turn back to the young faces, and not let on about what had happened.

On the ride home, I found a million reasons to blame myself for Thalia's distress. If I blamed myself, then there was something I could do to improve her quality of life. I could get her a quieter ride next time, or carry her gently into the building, or insist the children sit even more still. Ultimately, I understood that there was nothing I could do to ensure Thalia's comfort, but I still was not ready to give up.

Within a few nights of this heartbreaking experience, I had a terribly disturbing dream.

I went and got Thalia out to show her to my grandma. Instead, a long battle ensued. Thalia kept getting off the glove and I'd have to yank her around by her jesses to get her back on. First we were outside by a puddle of water and some reeds, then we were in a shopping mall. Regardless, the struggle got increasingly intense as she began to foot me anywhere she could. She started to bite me too. It hurt very badly. Soon enough I was just trying to hold her legs with both hands, but she was so strong and extremely angry that she kept getting away from me. As I walked into a huge sporting goods store, I had Thalia struggling in my arms. I felt my frustration level rising. The sales clerk said "Oh great! That would be wonderful if you could show her to all those people back there waiting." Her words were absolutely ridiculous. Then we came to a long row of lockers. I swung Thalia around a few times by her legs to try and confuse her to gain control. I worried that I would break her legs. I opened up the locker where she was to go. Thalia had a strong grip on me. She dug her talons into my stomach. Somehow I pried her loose and shoved her in the locker. I was mindful to make sure her leash wasn't in with her to get tangled up in.

Even after waking up and shaking the dreamtime, the anger Thalia held against me in the dream was overwhelming. I felt guilty enough as it was, but now I was beyond remorse. In my attempt to control her environment and provide her with a safe, comfortable life, I had ended up in a full out battle with her. Our struggle had moved from the spiritual setting of the outdoors (puddle and reeds) to a physical grappling in ordinary reality (fight in the shopping mall). At first I focused on the spiritual and emotional issues brought up during our time together walking Willow Brook's grounds such as the case of healing the wounds of my sexual assault. At some point when Thalia was turned over entirely to my care, my intent turned to controlling the physical aspects in her reality. I was doing everything I could think of within the constraints of the human world to try and make our relationship work. The symbology of the sporting goods store was apt. I was seeking out games to distract myself from the gut-wrenching work Thalia and I were capable of doing together. The stark contrast between our deep, soulful encounters and the painstakingly ordinary experience of justifying our livelihood to civilized folk was too hard to reconcile. I was angry that I had to work to prove our worth rather than just live it. I was trying to lock all of this turmoil away from others (stuffing Thalia in the locker). That morning, I journeyed on the dream to see what other insight I could gain.

I traveled to lower world and met with a red-tailed hawk. She confirmed that Thalia initiated the anger cycle I witnessed in the dream, but that I was cycling it back to her through my own anger. She told me that I had an opportunity to move the anger out of the circle to aid in Thalia's healing. I could do this by moving it through my body and releasing it into the ground. I asked the red-tail and a bear that had arrived to please show me where Thalia's anger came from. I saw the harrier, who was about fledgling age. Her talons were going at a person's face as the person was trying to restrain her. Then, because the person felt threatened, they put pressure on Thalia. I understood that this may have been when her wing was still healing. This was the point when Thalia learned that she would be injured for defending herself. She lost her sense of appropriate aggression. My power animals agreed to bring back this soul part for Thalia.

Next, I saw a downy creamy harrier nestling pinned to the ground as a haying machine went over her nest. Thalia thought that she was going to die in that moment. I learned that a large chunk of her spirit did die that day, and that now it was coming back to be with her.

There was more that the red-tailed hawk wanted to share with me, but I insisted on wrapping things up because I was exhausted. She traveled with me back to middle world to Thalia's mews. I stayed just long enough to see that the soul parts were delivered to her and then returned home.

I finally had an answer why Thalia was pulling her feathers. She learned early in life that defending herself brought her serious physical injury. She had omitted lashing out at someone from the loop and went directly to mutilating herself when threatened. This is common in human psychology. As adults, abused children often assault their bodies with drugs and reckless behavior.

The same day I did this journeywork I moved Thalia to a large flight cage. This mews was more exposed to the elements and visible to wild animals on the grounds. I had given up trying to control every aspect of her life. I was giving up control of every aspect of my own. I was scared to death I would lose her. I was terrified I would lose myself.

Instead of fussing over feeding times, avoiding traumatic stimuli, and trying to quell rage and fear, I turned my energy and worry over to the spirits.

In the womb of my tree I saw a spider. There was another black being with me. I squinted to try and identify it. The spider was small and unassuming, so I searched harder in the womb to identify the darkness. Then I felt the soft fur and saw the yellow eyes of a black panther. I knew it was there for Thalia, so I invited the cat to lower world to travel with me. I told her that at the end of the journey I could bring her back as a power animal for Thalia if that is what she wanted. The panther wanted to come with me. I traveled to lower world and met the black panther, my cougar, a red-tailed hawk, and a barn owl. My horse showed up and followed us. I asked, "What healing is in Thalia's best interest at this time?"

My power animals led me to a cave. I knelt at the opening before entering. Both the barn owl and the red-tailed hawk flew off into the darkness at the back of the cave. The cougar, one of my main power animals, and the panther rolled around in the dirt. They chased each other and generally had a great time playing together. I was waiting for the owl and hawk to return with a healing and having a hard time concentrating with all of the commotion from the big cats. I asked them to stop, but the panther told me that I needed to learn how to work with distractions.

"Don't assume you know what's best for me," I responded to the black cat. Then they went back to playing. I got the sense that Thalia and I had been in a bit of a "cat fight" ourselves. This helped me drop the heavy guilt around my dance of anger with Thalia and see it instead as a healthy way of working out our differences and coming into agreement. We were here to do soul work together, not change the world one education program at a time.

Then out of the darkness came a soul part of Thalia's, flying at me crooked and off balance. I asked why she left; she told me she had gotten lost. There was too much confusion about how to feel and she just plain lost her way. She said she would come back and bring the gift of a right to be carefree for Thalia. A couple other soul parts presented themselves and agreed to come back and be with Thalia. One brought back joy, another delivered the water element, and a third carried the beauty and grace of the huntress's spirit.

While I was talking with the soul parts, the panther and cougar raced around me in a blur of darkness and light. I stopped briefly to acknowledge the message they conveyed. The dance that Thalia and I were engaged in involved cycles of joy and grief, health and pain, consciousness and denial. Every turn around the circle released deeper levels of light and shadow and was profoundly cleansing.

The black panther asked to come back and be a power animal for Thalia. She traveled with me and my power animals to be delivered directly to Thalia along with the soul parts.

In *Medicine Cards*, Jamie Sams and David Carson write the following about black panther: "Black panther's medicine allows humans to face their fears and dark behaviors, exploring those internal shadowy aspects of being. . . . Darkness is the place for seeking and finding answers, for accepting healings, and for accessing the hidden light of truth. . . . She shows us how to . . . fearlessly face the unknown. . . . If you are out of balance, your shadow may be creating demons of fear. Enter the stillness and refuse to surrender your personal authority to avoidance mechanisms, justifications, or mental gymnastics . . . tell your shadow to get lost! Then acknowledge and release any feelings of discomfort."

By now I had almost entirely set aside any training exercises with Thalia. If I did work with her on the glove, it was in her mews on her terms. She could either come to me over and over again to eat her meal one bite at a time or she could decide to sit quietly on her perch while I left the food for her. Along with the journeying I was doing with Thalia, I was still working with Galena on my own issues on a regular basis. We were working on healing a myriad of soul losses, from the fear I encountered when my femur broke at age eleven, to the anxiety I wrestled with during my parent's divorce. In tandem with this healing work, Galena was teaching me how to work with intention and, thus, manifest in my life. This gave me a new format to work with. I had an alternative to the nausea of endless cover letters and a never-finished resume. I could spend an hour or two getting clear about what I wanted regardless of what I thought I could get, write these wishes down on paper, and journey to gather the power I needed to bring my true desires into the world. With that work done, I could carry on the business of living.

About a month after I accepted the job at the farm, I accepted a part-time position as a vet tech at Willow Brook. The vision I had in my heart was coming into being. On a daily basis, I came into contact with handfuls of new animals. Each had their own story and brought their own teaching into my life. I was able to use my soft hands to help undo what a careless human had done. I was able to use my open heart to carry through whatever message each animal had to offer. My spiritual transformation began to accelerate. As I worked to help heal each individual, the stories the animals carried healed another part of me. I was able to honor my spirit guides by meticulously caring for their incarnate counterparts. Ordinary reality and the spirit realm began to blend. There was still one unfinished piece: my relationship with Thalia.

I often wondered what the purpose of her life was, why she had been in servitude to humans despite her best efforts, and why we seemed destined to meet. It slowly became more and more evident that Thalia's time in this world was short. I decided to do a life purpose journey for her to learn the most during the time we had.

I was standing on the runway of the island, saddened by the silence, with my horse, cougar, and black panther. There were no harriers there now. We all walked to the point I used to visit every morning to look over the harbor. There I sat on some rocks and looked over the ocean. Thalia came and stood next to me, perched on the rocks. I cried cleansing tears for a short time, then turned to look over my shoulder. Thalia had moved. She was perched atop the solid rock cross that marked a Spanish conquistador's claiming of the island for his country. Panther looked over at me and told me that this was the symbol of Thalia's life purpose—her standing on that cross. Panther also told me that I had brought the wild back to the spirit of the island with the coming of the harriers and that I must now bring back the wild to a harrier spirit.

I wondered if the panther had things inside out and backwards. The harriers brought the wild back to the spirit of the island, and this harrier was bringing back the wild to my own spirit. Maybe he worded things this way for a reason. I was starting to see that this story was woven tighter than I thought. I was the spirit of the island, I was a wild harrier, I was Thalia, and she was me. She was the spirit of the island trapped under the whims of conquistadors, ranchers, and careless human beings. She was the spirit of the island that could never be owned. She was a wild northern harrier that flew over oceans. She was a quiet woman buried under the guise of human civilization, a system that staked a claim on her own soul. The story of her release from human conquest was my story of liberation.

One night I dreamt that I was going to the mouth of Willow Canyon on the island. I had tried this while living on the island during the summer solstice two years before and stopped short because of my fears of walking right out of this world and away from my family. In the dream, I ended up stuck in exactly the same place I'd gotten stuck in two years before. But then, I saw a course up and out of either side of the canyon via a huge stair step of boulders. I stood there, trying to decide if this was a safe way to go. I worried I might hurt myself and not make it back. Then, like magic, I was able to see the ocean in front of me. I didn't move my feet, but the distant view of the shore slowly transformed into the mouth of the canyon. I was on the beach, which was made of black, round stones. They sounded like a symphony in their tumbling, rushing, and rolling with each wave against the shore. There were elephant seals watching me at the edge of the surf. Off to my left I saw a tall cliff jutting straight up out of the ocean, probably eight hundred feet up. My husband Chris was there with me too. I looked back behind us and spotted three short-eared owls, one adult and two young. I was pointing them out to Chris when the piece of land they were on turned into a floating fragment of earth. It floated right behind us and away.

When I was hiking down Willow Canyon alone during the summer solstice I was firmly entrenched in fear. Partway down the canyon, I froze almost in tears and promptly climbed out of the canyon to return to my cabin. In the dream, I was given a second chance to overcome my fears and hike to the mouth of the canyon in safety. This time around I didn't take the chance to leave (stair step of boulders), but decided to stay and do the spiritual work. I was promptly rewarded as the shore came to me. To my ultimate surprise and delight, my husband was there with me. The clear message in his company was that I didn't have to leave my family to realize my dream of living outside the system, of living like the wild ones.

The tall cliff in the distance was a reminder that I didn't realize my fear of falling off the edge or going insane. I had found safe passage to the shore. In *Animal Speak* by Ted Andrews, seals are acquainted with active imagination, creativity, and lucid dreaming. They were a clear representation of the shamanic journeywork I had been doing. The black, round stones made a sound that resonated with my soul. Each of these stones represented an issue I was working on that was constantly being polished. Each evolved through the working of the tides. The short-eared owls reminded me of the mystery, always in the background that exists outside of time and space (floating chunk of land). It seemed that every time I ran into these owls, I couldn't find them again. They were always a mirage. In their elusiveness they seemed to say, "Follow me just a little bit further into the great mystery beyond."

The great mystery was calling Thalia and she was answering. She wasn't responding to my calls to the glove as frequently and was uncharacteristically interested in hanging out on the ground of her mews. One afternoon when I found her on the ground, I threw her food to her and she thrust out her leg to grab it greedily in her talons.

Then the hawk walked to a patch of grass that she had carefully stomped into a nest. There she stood with her wings spread over her meal and her neck arched down. I could feel the muscles in her neck stretching. From her throat came a low call, much like that of an eagle or red-tailed hawk yelling down from the heavens. I reveled in her gift, grateful for my dear friend's inner voice and flattered by her answer to my request made so long ago.

There were other signs that she was dancing near the veil between this world and those beyond. She regressed further into feather pulling, sometimes for obvious reasons, and other times for no apparent reason. On lawn mowing days I'd find a fresh pile of down drifting on the gravel of her mews. Other days I'd look down and notice that her legs were more bare than the day before.

I began finding great horned owl feathers in and around her mews and hearing their haunting hoots when I'd go to feed Thalia late in the day. Something about the presence of the owls was foreboding. It was like finding scraps of the grim reaper's cloak or hearing his breath on the wind.

The ongoing conversation between Ian, Sandra, Annie, and I had come to a conclusion. Thalia would be euthanized. I was given the choice of when. I choose the longest day of the year, a time of celebration of the light and moving once again towards the darkness. Her last day would be the summer solstice.

On Thalia's final full day on this planet, I walked into the large flight cage now overgrown with weeds and tall grass, took a timid, live mouse out of a box, and showed it to the harrier. She watched intently as I walked across her mews to the stump and placed the white mouse down by his tail. I barely took one step back before she was on top of it. Her toes were wrapped snug but careful around the mouse. He looked up at me as if to say, "I'm trapped," but I saw no signs of pain in his eyes. I looked at his sweet face, then up at her confident one. She let go of the mouse for a split second. He ran to leap off the edge of the stump and in a flash he was in her grasp, squeaking in pain. The hawk clenched hard.

Unlike other raptors I knew, she didn't proceed to ravenously tear at the shaking body. She stood stoic over the struggling soul, honoring the life sacrificed to extend her own. Time folded in on itself. I can't imagine how long we stood there because we had slipped into another realm. I could feel the hawk's spirit lift off with the spirit of the mouse in her talons. She was carrying the soul of her prey to the afterlife. It had never occurred to me before this moment that hawks, as hunters, could possess this special gift. From my earth-bound, anthropocentric viewpoint I hadn't ever stopped to wonder how a hawk related to the spirit of her prey at the time of the kill. For me, this experience dispelled the idea of the greedy, mindless killing machine. There was much more than the flow of the food chain going on here. This was not just mouse meat becoming hawk flesh. This was a mouse offering its body and the hawk offering the mouse passage to another world in return.

While our consciousness returned to the cage, the late sun's horizontal rays split through the oak trees and cage walls. We stood quietly as the mouse's muscles grew soft. I watched Thalia's entire body language shift. Pride radiated from her. Tears began streaming down my cheeks. I thought of how good a mother she would have been. Her fiery aggression and deadly swiftness would have protected many healthy, well-fed young. I cried that she hadn't gotten to be the terror of the marsh, afraid of no one. I cried because this box and these pony tricks had been her life.

She looked down at the limp mouse warm in her grip and then glanced up at me. I understood that she was asking for solitude. She wouldn't eat a freshly killed meal in my company. I didn't ask why, but rather left her to her wild ways.

I quietly slipped out the door to allow her to eat in peace and set to leisurely pacing the grounds. I could feel the dampness of the night start to creep in. A wild great horned owl hooted overhead. I peered into the dense canopy, unable to pick up the winged one with the haunting voice. Softly I carried on past the cages neighboring Thalia's to check in on the education birds or recovering animals within. I was well into my time as a vet tech at Willow Brook and was at least partly responsible for the welfare of every animal there. Like a mother with a litter of newborns, I always had my eyes and ears open for signs of trouble. As I turned to watch the mallards paddling in their pool, I caught the sight of struggle in the corner of my eye. Between the screen and wire in the wall of an empty cage was a fury of scrambling black, white, and rust-colored feathers. Eerie, blood red eyes were full of panic. I quickly moved closer and recognized the captured bird as a spotted towhee. He was struggling to find his way out of the mess he'd somehow gotten himself into.

Spotted towhees reside in thickets and are regularly heard scratching under leaves for insects, seeds, or fruits. Given their proclivity for the underbrush, these large members of the sparrow family have an innate knack for squeezing through tight spots. Apparently, this bird had found a hole in the screen and wormed his way in. I searched everywhere, but could not find the opening he used. He couldn't seem to find it either.

I put my falconry equipment in a pile on the ground and hurried up to the clinic for some tools. I returned five minutes later with a pry bar and was able to rip off the wood strip that held the screen in place. With a little bit of nudging towards the opening, the towhee was set free.

His wings burst forth in a cacophony of sound. I felt the waves of release hit my body as he flew off. Then I noticed that someone was watching me. I turned around and looked across the lawn into Thalia's mews. She stared back, head cocked to one side. In that moment I understood. In her ceremony for the mouse, the hawk had honored what I was doing for her own spirit. In my rescue of the towhee, I had paid tribute to what she was doing for mine.

~

PART TWO

Gracious One

~

☞ 7 ☜

Game of Owl and Mouse

After losing Thalia there was a great sense of relief. Her spirit was free and so was mine. No longer did I fret every day about the walls caging her in, and the dreadful role I played in holding her there. The box of modern society and cultural frivolities no longer held me captive. I now moved through my days with only my gut to guide me. This kind of self-assurance is assuredly self-love. When you are a gift to yourself everything shifts, sparkles, and glows around you. I had the gift of the moment, overjoyed with what was moving through me, grateful for the visions that came. Before, I had been living mainly in my head in the land of reactivity. Now I was living more like the wild ones.

A barn owl does not stop in mid-flight through the night sky and think, "Why is it I can see through the dark? Is it best that I do so? How do I use this gift?" The barn owl just sees in the dark and knows how to do so very well. The mouse that the barn owl is hunting doesn't sense the owl descending upon her with talons open and think, "What do I do about that owl? Where do I have to hide? I wonder what the owl is doing?" The mouse moves to her burrow right before she senses the owl descending.

There is mostly action in the wild world. Reaction dominates the human world.

It felt like I was standing on the island on the top of Green Mountain, surrounded by fields of tall grass with the island laid underneath me. All was stunning and worrisome at the same time. I was completely and hopelessly alone. Sure, the harriers and ravens would look over at me as they flew past my shoulder from time to time, and the songs of meadowlarks wafted up to me from the valley below, but ultimately I was of no consequence in their lives. If I were to go back to the mainland and sink into the comfortable blanket of depressed denial once again, the harriers wouldn't mind—neither would the ravens. They had their own business to go about, catching mice and raiding nests. Summer was well underway and they were obligated to take advantage of the short season before the cold fog of winter came back to the island.

During the months following the summer solstice I took up caring for Willow Brook's resident barn owl Rhett, or Papa Rhett as I lovingly came to refer to him. He'd been at the center for five years, and begrudgingly obliged the absurd request of his handlers to go out on walks in the middle of the day. When I'd go into his mews to ask him onto my glove he'd slowly bend his head down at me and gradually open his eyes to narrow slants from his high perch. Clearly, I was a disruption to his precious sleep and he wouldn't have minded if I'd gone about my day without stepping foot on his island. I think that's why I came to calling him Papa Rhett. He had that lofty air of a working father, the man that's so tired from a day's hard work that he seems to groan when his family begs for his attention. After much coaxing and sleeve tugging, the dad then gets up out of his recliner and follows his little girl to her room to see her latest painting, and, under the cover of exhaustion, he smiles. Ultimately, she is his world, but at the end of the day you'd never know it. That was Papa Rhett.

I took to caring for this crabby owl because, to be honest, it seemed he had no friends. His handler of three years had recently moved away, and Papa Rhett had a different person on his schedule every day of the week. I could relate to that and thought maybe we could offer each other some much longed-for company. I could walk in the hole that had been left by his former handler, and he could stand in the chasm that had been left by my beloved hawk. We'd replaced a male handler with a female handler and a female hawk with a male owl. The exchange was odd from the start. For days on end there was this unnerving tension between us. I waffled back and forth between my desire for companionship and my complete distrust that anyone would ever want to accompany me along my path of discovery.

With his body language, Rhett seemed to mirror the same experience. One moment he would glare at me and chatter some rubbish, as if to say, "How dare you think you can talk to an owl like me?" The next moment he would take to delicately preening a long flight feather on the end of his wing. His head would gracefully twist sideways as his beak carefully zipped and caressed the barbs of the feather into place. I was swept away in the ballet of the moment until he noticed himself, turned to glare at me, and stomped his foot on the glove.

"Oh yes, that's right, Rhett, how dare I fall in love with you," I'd adoringly chuckle. And I did—fall in love with him, that is.

Over time I learned when to sidestep his grumpiness and when to meet it head on. We spent hours in the corridor of green grass that lay between the cages on the property. There he'd fly from my glove to the perch stationed at the far end of the lawn. I've been told that owls, for reasons I have yet to speculate on, prefer to fly from the glove to the perch, while hawks prefer the opposite routine. This reversal of roles was healing for me. I had to learn how to communicate to the owl that I was ready to let go, rather than beg him and bait him with food to come to me.

This letting go part was easier said than done. It took me weeks of standing with him on the glove, staring at the perch and waiting. The antics I went through to try and convince him to fly were, I'm sure, absolutely hysterical to onlookers. He seemed to gather the most pleasure out of watching me dance, cajole, coax, and whine. *Certainly, there must be some key movement or cue that I'm just not doing right or at all*, I convinced myself, and continued on with the arm waving and gibberish talking. It's hard to tell what spirits I cursed or conjured or plain offended, but I just couldn't get that sticky owl off my glove. This, keep in mind, was the same owl who apparently despised stepping onto my glove at the beginning of every session.

Eventually, though, my persistence paid off and, paradoxically, I was able to let go. Letting go didn't just entail that I release his leash, point, and say "perch," because I'd done that dozens of times before with no results. This was an entirely different way of working in the world. On this occasion, like magic, as I turned to face the perch I felt the cells in my body relax and tingle. As I opened my fingers to release my hold on his tether I felt energy lift up through my hand. As I raised my right hand to point to the perch I felt my intent and focus carry me to the perch, and without hesitation Rhett's stare locked in on his destination and he lifted off. I stood, jaw dropped, and watched him glide like an angel inches above the blades of grass. Then with a whimsical flutter of the tips of his wings he lifted up and lighted quietly on the perch. Every time he left my glove from that moment forward, I had the same transcendental experience. In this way, my friend by default supported me in holding on to the lessons Thalia had brought me. By teaching me how to let go, Papa Rhett was teaching me how to consistently embrace the unknown and live in the moment. Like the wild barn owl descending on a mouse, I was probing into the night with outstretched talons, ready to grab whatever opportunity, whatever nourishment the moment held for me. Like a wild deer mouse collecting seeds under the cover of darkness, I was hyperaware of my surroundings should a hungry barn owl fly overhead.

I was busy those summer months caring for the sick, injured, and orphaned animals that came into Willow Brook as well as working weekends at the organic farm. Most of my journal entries from that time involved either dreams or waking reality encounters with the wide spectrum of animals I attended to. There was little time for shamanic journeying and I was so overwhelmed with information from just the dreams and daily events that I was barely able to record what I held in the palms of my hands. Ink and paper seemed the safest place to share my stories, because as Papa Rhett and I spent more time together our interactions became more and more otherworldly.

Now that I had learned to let go and had fallen in love with our time in the corridor lawn, Rhett was no longer interested in flying. That doesn't mean I didn't try to make it happen, but his persistent stare towards the back of the wildlife center's property and his incredulous stubbornness about leaving the glove forced me to oblige his promptings. One afternoon, instead of walking him over and leashing him up for flying, I followed his gaze. We walked past the raccoon cages and over the small bridge. As we came to the second to last cage, Rhett's head snapped to our right and his eyes fixed on the young skunk inside. For minutes his stare didn't waver. This may not seem of any consequence, but this picky barn owl rarely ventured to show interest in much of anything. It was part of the tough guy routine he used to avoid showing attachment.

Since my wide-faced companion stood so still, I turned from watching him watch the skunk to actually watching the skunk myself. The sweet little one had stopped drinking from his water bowl and lifted his tail in response to our intrusion upon his quiet evening. He took to walking in lazy circles, stopping as he passed closest to us to put his front paws up on the screen of the cage and sniff the air that carried our scent to him. After three or four passes, his tail dropped to horizontal and he went back to lapping water from his bowl. There was no mistake in Papa Rhett directing me to the far reaches of Willow Brook's property. The cages out there were the most secluded and private of all. Just beyond them was where Thalia and I had stood in the meadow. Out there I felt safe to look into other worlds without interruption or judgment. Like this skunk who had dropped his guard, I was no longer caught up in worry over my reputation.

Papa Rhett and I shared a handful of other experiences similar to this one, and they became the sacred cow in our relationship. The stubborn owl would insist I stand still and stare into some cage, and if I began to doubt or pull away he would respond fiercely by stomping on the glove, glaring at me, and sometimes even jumping off the glove. He communicated displeasure through his behavior whenever I dismissed these experiences or worried that someone would see me. In this way, the tension in our relationship never waned. The battles were never really with the standoffish owl that apparently enjoyed my company; he was just doing me the favor of mirroring my internal turmoil.

In the fading days of that summer, I yearned with every cell in my body for the companionship of a hawk. Some would say I was just trying to fill the gaping hole left by a nervous harrier. Others might remark that I had some delusion that I have a soul connection to the tribe of the hawks. I could guess that I wasn't satisfied in other areas of my life or that I wasn't happy with myself or that I wanted a chance to show I could have a calm hawk on my glove. All of these doubts ate at me for weeks on end. I fulfilled my shamanic promptings to heal these doubts and met with Galena to have a soul retrieval about these issues. She not only brought back a deep well of soul parts, but also my dear friend Thalia as a power animal. I went home to visit my parents and spent time healing more parts of my relationship with them. In my search to find myself outside the world I knew before Thalia, I reconnected with many aspects of my younger self. Around the fall equinox, I went on a thirty-mile backpacking trip with my husband and sat aligning with the wilderness. After weeks of challenging inner work, my longing for a hawk stood strong. My final choice was to follow my heart, and the path to my new companion was fraught with more loss, grief, and doubt.

With Thalia gone, the raptor education program was without a hawk, and we all agreed the program was not complete. After many conversations and deliberations the center's director and education program's director agreed to allow me to take on training a new juvenile red-tailed hawk that fall. This was all contingent on us admitting a hawk that was fit to live in captivity but not equipped to live in the wild. This put me, as well as the others, in a moral bind. Of course we wanted every animal that passed through Willow Brook's doors to be released into the wild, but there is a sensitive time while an animal is recovering when no one really knows the outcome. No one knows whether the animal will return to full health and be able to support itself in the wild again, whether it will heal enough to live comfortably in captivity, or whether the animal's injury will never completely mend.

On my walk into the wildlife center one morning, Ian Whitham, the director, met me on his front porch. In his arms he held a box with a juvenile red-tail standing inside. My heart skipped and I confessed to myself that it was hard not to let the thought of "education bird" slip into my mind. Ian asked me to take the bird down to the clinic, but my arms were full with the carrier of the northern flicker (a woodpecker) chick I was raising. I continued down to the clinic and began my rounds for the day. Soon thereafter, I was standing with Ian in the treatment room as he pulled the gorgeous beast out of the cardboard box. The hawk looked at us through her clear, bright eyes, calmly accepting our restraint. We held her on the table merely as a formality, as she didn't resist our hands for even a moment. Sometimes an animal's sheer volume of pain, hunger, and thirst sends them into an eerie shock. This hawk was obviously separated from the experience in some way—she didn't fight for her life, but the stare in her eyes told of an abysmal strength and knowing. Her stare held a powerful life force like that of a courageous warrior entering into the battle of his fateful undoing.

Inspection of the hawk's injuries pointed to electrocution. She was missing five or so flight feathers from her left wingtip. A fairly large, crusty wound was where feathers once were. She likely flew into a power line with her left wing and the electricity arched out of her left foot, which was now badly swollen. Ian predicted that there would be a die-off of tissue, but also a good chance that the hawk would recover from her injuries and be able to live comfortably in captivity. We moved her into a small wooden cage in the ICU and left her with some food. Ian was leaving on vacation in a few hours, so I took instructions on when and how to start hand-feeding the hawk. Already, I was struggling with the aching feeling in my heart, and how badly I wanted to love this courageous bird. I felt powerless to hold back the love that was streaming from my being. I wished I could remain detached. I wished I could let myself flow through my heart.

When I returned to the wildlife center to care for the red-tail that evening I found her sitting quietly in her cage with two mice at her feet. My heart sank. If she wouldn't eat, the prognosis was dreadful. I realized she might be too far gone. She could be in the core of a battle, with the only way out being death. I decided to ask my dear friend Papa Rhett for help.

I didn't know what Rhett could or would do, but he was the only one I knew to turn to. I thawed and packed up three mice for the owl and headed outside in the last light of day. As I approached Rhett's mews I saw his white underside against the wall. He was hanging to the cage by his talons, wings partly outstretched, staring in my direction. I was completely stunned. Rhett rarely antici-pated my approach and he had never been so anxious to meet me. When I walked into his mews it became plainly obvious that Rhett was looking for food. In our few months of working together he'd never requested or eaten food from my hands. He would take food occasion-ally from a couple of his other handlers while they worked with him, but he always refused food from me. I had tried enough times that I'd actually given up on the idea that he'd ever dine on my glove.

This time, he practically leapt onto my glove and leaned towards the pouch of food on my hip while I put on his leash. I resisted his plea for food until we were out-side of his mews. He snatched the mouse from my fingers like he hadn't eaten in days, even though I knew he'd had a meal every day leading up to this one. I watched him snap the mouse's neck, and surgically sever the head from the body. He threw his head back and gulped down the mouse head. Next he carefully opened the body cavity and delicately removed his favorite organs, one by one.

Raptor's beaks are commonly viewed as tearing and grabbing utensils. This barn owl used his beak like a scal-pel and tweezers. His precision was remarkable. He pro-ceeded to disconnect the torso from the hindquarters of the mouse and finish his meal in those two last bites. I stood captivated, relieved to watch him eat. The expe-rience was truly cathartic. Halfway up to the clinic, we stopped and I fed Rhett a second mouse. He took even more time to consume this mouse. I did my best to remain patient. My friend seemed to have a plan.

Once in the door of the clinic, Rhett took to star-ing towards the ICU. I did my best to hurry and prepare another mouse for the hungry owl. His gaze, in typical

Rhett fashion, was locked. I carried him into the ICU, reached over with my free hand, and lifted the sheet off of the door to the red-tail's cage. To my amazement, the hawk stood leaned over a mouse of her own, eating to her heart's content. She did not pause to look up at us. I was comforted to know our presence was not an intrusion. Once she finished her meal she looked up at us and calmly returned to an upright posture. I stood there with the barn owl on my glove staring into the eyes of this lovely bird. Tears welled in my eyes and I thanked both my feathered companions for the healing they had enacted. As a "thank you" to the red-tail I used my intention to send her my red-tailed hawk power animal. I had taken the leap of faith and now the magic in my world was in their talons.

Six days later, we had to euthanize the hawk. She gratefully accepted food from my hands every day until then, but the flesh on her wing continued to die off at an alarming rate. She eventually got a systemic infection and was suffering from a burning fever. The decision to put her down was by this time a welcome end. As I stood there with the sleeping bird lying on the treatment table before me, in my mind's eye I saw my power animal red-tail drift down, meld with the dying hawk's spirit, and carry her up out of her body to the heavens above. That was the only moment of peace I had for weeks. A week later, we admitted and euthanized a second red-tailed hawk that also had electrocution burn wounds on her left wing and foot. Now I was disturbed. Not only had these two red-tails come in with left wing injuries, but we also had a female osprey, a couple of rabbits, a female western tanager, and a female kingfisher with similar wounds. All of these animals eventually died or were euthanized.

I seemed to be dancing with an unsettling mystery—mystery related to power, death, and the feminine. The left side of the body is commonly associated with the feminine. In *Mary Summer Rain's Guide to Dream Symbols* by Mary Summer Rain and Alex Greystone, "electrocution warns against the desire for power." I remarked to Ian one day during this deluge of bizarre events that I felt like mother death.

Thalia had led me along the path to both my and her own salvation. In the process of caring for each other our spirits were freed. Once my spirit was released from the confines of the ordinary world, Papa Rhett guided me into a true understanding of how to access and experience my free, wild knowing. I still longed for more because I had been living this wild way—my true way—in hiding, like the fox who disappears into the foliage. I'd cleverly learned to camouflage myself, but there was only so far I could go. The mouse who lives in fear of the owl spends a considerable amount of her energy watching overhead. She has little attention left to pay to the marvelous details in front of her nose. I saw and lived all these details constantly, but I was too busy hiding my ability, and many messages were lost in the process. I yearned to direct my full attention to the way spirit moves through all things. I felt an overwhelming calling to gather these details, these messages from spirit, and bring them into the world. This was the same longing that called for a companion hawk.

Ultimately, I was searching to live my full feminine power. I was asking for a new guide to show me the way. In my search for a guide, my fear of power and my antiquated definition of it needed to die. That was the message these animals with left wing injuries were bringing through. I was misled to believe that power involved control, manipulation, and abuse. None of these qualities were in my nature. I didn't want any of these to factor into my relationship with a red-tailed hawk. I worked hard to wash away these misconceptions and replace them with a new definition of empowerment.

In the end, it was a game of owl and mouse that brought me fully into understanding. As I struggled one evening with my fear of power and longing for the same, I fumbled with Rhett in the corridor lawn. I set up a three-ring circus of perches and tried flying him to or from either one. In the process, I got tangled up in his leash and thoroughly irritated him. I kept trying to offer him a mouse during the games, but he refused to buy into the web I was weaving.

"It seems impossible," I thought to myself. "How can I train a red-tailed hawk to live in captivity and to resist her wild urge to flee without controlling, manipulating, or abusing her? It seems absolutely impossible. I can't seem to live without this hawk, but I also couldn't live with myself should I ever harm her in any way."

Finally, I gave up. I stood still, holding a mouse on my glove and waiting for Rhett to come to me. After a very long silence, he was on my glove. Rhett rarely came to my glove for food. He stood over the mouse, holding it for what seemed the longest time. I began to seethe with frustration. Why wouldn't he eat the damn mouse? Then, feeling like an absolute blockhead, I realized that he was trying to tell me something. In that same instant, he jumped off of my glove and onto the ground. I had let go of the situation so absolutely that I hadn't grabbed his leash in my hand. My foot was still firmly planted on the leash, so I was not worried he'd get away. Instead, I turned to reading his message while kneeling before him, asking him to step onto the glove.

"Okay, what does mouse mean? Details. All right, but what does that matter?" I thought.

Rhett moved the mouse into his beak and stepped onto my glove. He turned his back to me and spread his wings over the mouse. Clearly, he was guarding the mouse from me like a wolf hovering over its kill. He was intent on doing so because he had to carefully hold his balance while standing sideways on the glove.

"He's guarding, hoarding the details, but from what?" I asked. He kept glancing around nervously.

"What is he looking for?" I asked myself. Then, responding to my own question, I said, "Oh yeah, he's looking out for great horned owls. He's shielding the details from those who might hoot them out into the world like frivolous gossip, thus eradicating them on the scene."

Rhett immediately turned 180 degrees around to face me and began eating the mouse. Bingo! That was the message. What ensued was the longest dinner yet. He ate little bit by little bit, just barely taking any meat in each bite. A little rib here. A taste of thigh meat. Half a kidney. It was a meal of details. Clearly the message here was to honor, sustain, and protect the medicine of mouse.

Mice seemed to frequently accompany me on my path. I'd trapped and handled hundreds of them on the island. My first shamanic journey was solely about an interaction with a sweet and friendly mouse. While volunteering and working at Willow Brook, I was constantly feeding mice to a host of raptors. My first patient as a vet tech was a deer mouse who I later released, healthy, into the wild.

All mouse has is what's right in front of her nose. Therefore, she must work from humility. It's this sense that I am only a small piece of the cosmic order of things that was able to bring me into a place of acceptance. My yearning to work with a red-tailed hawk was what it was, judgment-free. But, as Rhett had shown me, I had to carefully guard my dream. Before this experience I had ached endlessly for outside validation in my quest for a new feathered friend, but this was my spiritual path, no one else's. Rhett reminded me to honor the sacred womb time before my vision was birthed out into the world and to not share it prematurely out of doubt or lack of self-esteem.

❧ 8 ❧

Out of Hiding

On a sunny morning in mid-September, Ian led me into the ICU to introduce me to our next education program candidate. The juvenile red-tailed hawk stood in the small wooden cage, alert and comfortable in her surroundings. She was in beautiful condition, so lovely that the white feathers on her upper chest were practically glowing. Her yellow eyes eagerly glared back at us. Curiosity was written all over her face. There was reason to pause, though, as I noticed her right wing was sagging.

Ian explained that the hawk had a dislocated elbow. He reminded me that bird bones heal remarkably fast and there is only a window of a couple hours during which breaks and dislocations can be reset. Otherwise, the bones start to grow and fix in the broken position. Ian went on to say that we hadn't gotten this hawk quickly enough and that there was no way to repair her elbow. My heart ached for her, as I knew she would never soar again. In her short five or six months of life she'd done all the soaring she'd ever know in this body. There was no telling how her elbow would heal and how she might adapt and move with the handicap. She seemed incredibly comfortable around people. Was this the volunteer we'd been waiting for?

I continued with the duties of my day, bringing food to the animals at the center, washing dishes, and cleaning cages. Toward the end of the morning, as I walked the road back up to the clinic from the outdoor pens, I tipped back my head, my attention brought up into the glaring, bright blue. *That was a red-tailed hawk call.* Three hawks soared above me, talking back and forth to one another in a friendly banter. They danced in a circle under, over, and beside one another. The warm breeze of the day gave them plenty of excuse to enjoy the gift of flight. I thought of the two electrocuted hawks that had come before and the hawk that sat patiently in the ICU. I hadn't seen or heard wild red-tailed hawks around the property for months.

In the afternoon, I spent some time sitting in the ICU with the hawk, patiently waiting for her to eat the dead chicks in her cage. She was more interested in watching me and the young turkey vulture in the cage behind me. Sometimes she stared right at me for minutes on end, studying every line in my face, and other times she looked straight through me. I wondered what she saw behind me and guessed it was the turkey vulture.

I returned to visit her that evening and found that she had eaten in my absence. She stood still, intensely watching my every move as I gently placed a mouse on the perch beside her feet. Ian and I paused in the ICU for a while, contemplating this bird. She examined us with the same intent. We speculated about whether she was male or female, but mostly we wondered what the world looked like from behind her eyes. We talked about writing stories from the perspective of a raptor, but admitted that we'd never really quite know what they saw. At the time it felt better left a mystery.

We moved on to discussing various names for the hawk. In a glimmer of hope and magic, I thought "Isabeau" from the movie *Ladyhawke*. By day she was a red-tailed hawk, by night she was a woman. By day her lover was a man, by night he was black wolf. They'd been cursed to their opposing existence by a jealous bishop. The movie is the story of how they broke the spell and came into human form together. When I saw this movie as a child I absolutely fell in love. This was my first exposure to the art of falconry. The man with the hawk on his glove and the woman the hawk embodied captivated me. Obviously, to name this hawk in the light of my childhood visions and dreams would carry a strong magic. I was hesitant to make such a strong commitment, knowing that ultimately she "belonged" to the wildlife center and to a life of service. To name her in my image would inseparably link us in a way I wasn't sure I was allowed or safe to do. I also used the excuse that we didn't know her gender to dismiss my yearning.

The best bet was to pick a neutral name. Ian, following my lead, began to ponder the story of *Ladyhawke* and suggested the name "Mouse." In the movie, Mouse was a good-hearted pickpocket who got swept up in the love story and helped the couple break the spell over them. Ian thought it was a clever paradox to name a hawk "Mouse." Our eyes focused back on the hawk, watching us watch her. The red-tail stood brave with the limp mouse laid at her feet. Clearly, this formidable beast was nowhere near the embodiment of a timid rodent. We chuckled at his joke and went home for the evening.

The next evening I wrote in the hawk's care log:

"September 17, 7 p.m., Fed six mice from the glove!!! She was reaching out for the last few. Bending down to eat mice from talons (a sign of trust because she couldn't watch me while bent over). She preened a bit (another sign of comfort and trust) and let me touch her toes with my gloved hand. Very calm."

The hawk's training advanced quickly because she was very fond of food and she readily accepted our presence. She actually anticipated our coming and moved to us to get food. Her weight was low, so we fed her all she could eat for days. She absolutely gorged herself. She even accepted food from my glove immediately after I had to hold her in a towel and handle her for an exam. I was astounded at her willingness to take on her new role in life. Within a week of being admitted into the wildlife center, the hawk was stepping onto both my glove and that of the education program coordinator, Sandra. Using food, kindness, and compassion we had won this wild animal's trust. Unfortunately, the honeymoon didn't last long.

Since this was my first time "manning" a bird, I received endless lines of advice and instruction. In some cases the guidance was sorely needed and greatly appreciated, as I was clueless about what my options were. Other times the suggestions were in direct conflict with what my intuition called me to do. A week and a half into the hawk's stay at the wildlife center, Ian recommended the red-tail move forward in her training. He believed, like other falconers, that the only way a raptor was going to learn to fully accept the human world and all of its surprises was to purposefully expose the bird to everything imaginable as quickly as possible.

My opinion is one in an ocean of perspectives, but to me this way of training is much like the imposed breaking of a horse. This method, also known as "flooding," seems to focus on numbing an animal's spirit to keep them under control. It doesn't feel like asking them to join into partnership. During my own training in the education program, I was handed a piece of writing by a falconer. The author encouraged trainers to study the intricacies of "positive reward" training because he believed there was no way to use negative conditioning with raptors. He pointed out that you can't tell a raptor "No" or bop it on the nose like a puppy getting into the garbage, and he's right, but I believe there's more to the story.

In my mind and heart, taking a wild animal with a heightened sense of fight or flight and restraining her in situations she perceives as life-threatening is negative conditioning. When a bird tries to get away from a threat, she has the disturbing experience of being bound by her ankles to both the situation and the person. No amount of food or "positive reward" can distract her from her distress. Eventually the animal can no longer hold a heightened level of adrenaline and goes into a sort of shock from pure exhaustion. I believe the bird doesn't accept the situation or the person she's with, she just plain gives up.

Like a fox, I decided to blend into the background and not speak up about my true feelings around this issue. I didn't own the bird, I was new to training raptors, and I had only been volunteering and working at the center for a year and a half. In more ways than one, I was at the bottom of the totem pole and had little say in the matter. I figured it was best to just go along with what the director suggested. At the time, I had little room to argue for a quieter way because I hadn't a chance to find it. I had all my theories about how this exposure method would work out, but in the end I'd never seen it done. This would be a learning experience for both the hawk and me.

First we grabbed the red-tail and wrapped her in a towel to bring her into the treatment room. There we fit her jesses, checked her body condition, and gave her a vaccine. She was well fleshed out after the days of gorging and Ian suggested we cut back on her food. Her elbow was calloused and healed by then, so she wouldn't be able to do any more damage by flapping that wing. We discussed moving her to a larger cage and investing time in teaching her to fly to the glove for food to strengthen the muscles in that wing and prevent it from drooping further. We fit her with a hood like those used in falconry for centuries. Hoods cover the raptor's eyes and effectively send the bird into a quiet, calm state. Critical care, such as medical treatments and beak clipping, can be performed on a hooded bird without causing prolonged stress.

When the exam was complete, Ian decided it was time to see how the hawk responded to the outside world. While she was still hooded, he stood her up and got her to grip and stand firmly on his glove. Then he pulled off her hood. Up until this point, all the hawk ever knew of this man was that he'd handled her for a few exams. She'd never received food from him or touched foot onto his glove before. This was her first time in a room surrounded by people on all sides. All signs showed that she was terrified. Her hackles were up on the back of her head; she held her wings out at her sides and panted for breath. I hadn't seen her in this much panic before. She took a few leaps off of his glove and hung by her ankles each time. He had to help lift her back to an upright position with his free hand.

I'm sure I didn't ease the situation, as I stood there frozen in fear. I felt completely powerless to move her to a safe place. Ian asked me to take her onto my glove. She jumped away from us and hung by her ankles again as we made the transfer and righted her on my glove. I walked as quickly and quietly as I could to get us out of the clinic and away from the circle of people. She stayed with me as I carried her out the door, but her terror didn't subside once we were outdoors. She was just as afraid of me as she was of everything else. I felt miserable. All of the trust and patience I had offered her in the days preceding seemed lost in this one callous act. I made a sorry attempt to save face by hiding my misery until I could no longer bear to hold her in the experience. I walked her to her new cage, unleashed her, and put her on the perch. She stared at me with a glazed over look, still panting. For the first time since we'd started working together, she refused food. Seeing that I was doing more harm than good by standing with her, I hastily left her cage.

The young red-tail's new mews was a room inside a small barn. She had walls on three sides, a decent-sized window at perch level, and a screened-in skylight above. She could sit during the many hours of the day she had alone and watch the neighboring barnyard animals. Compared to the small wooden box she'd spent the last couple weeks in, her new home was bustling with activity. In there she had plenty of room to stretch out her legs and move away from anyone she viewed as a threat. The following day I spent a brief ten minutes in her cage. When I approached her she jumped away from me and fell to the ground. From there she clumsily flapped and scrambled her way back up to her perch. She did not calm down or show any interest in food. Ashamed of myself and the poor choices I'd made, I left her alone.

Like the shell-shocked red-tailed hawk that had just plummeted into a nightmare, my spirit was in disarray. I wanted to live, breathe, and act the wild way without having to hide, but this wasn't how I intended to come out of hiding. This wasn't how I wanted the hawk to step into her new role as an ambassador bird either. We were losing ourselves in the process. I needed to reframe my aching urgency to walk in the world as I was. I had to redefine the path we were on to save my relationship with this gorgeous beast. I knew we could prove to others that we would be of great service in the world. The road we now walked wasn't leading us there.

It was clear that I had lost all the trust that hawk ever had in me, and now I needed to pay my dues to win it back. Like a bashful mate who had clearly wounded her lover, I knelt there before this edgy hawk with my heart in my hands. A common piece of advice I had been handed during my time in the education program was, "Spend as much time with the birds as you can, even just sitting in their mews reading a book." I decided to try this method, hoping that the bird would eventually accept me back into her world. After all, it seemed that Thalia appreciated the hours I had spent quietly standing in her cage in a meditative calm. This idea of communing with an animal conjured up poetic images of Diane Fosey with the mountain gorillas or Jane Goodall with the chimpanzees. With just enough patience, one could find invitation into the wild world. With this particular hawk's personality I had mixed results.

Early the next morning, I went into the hawk's cage with my hands full of pencils and a notebook. I intended to draw meditatively while I sat in the back corner of her room. I hoped I would become so enraptured with the image I was creating that my nerves and attention would move to the page and away from her. I figured that once I forgot about her being in the room, she would calm down and go about her own business. I sat as quietly as I could while rhythmically coursing my pencils across the paper. I tried not to look up or stop breathing every time she acted like she was going to jump and hang off the bars in her window. When she panicked and was hanging off the window, I tried to ease my heart into the next beat. We went on in this manner for likely an entire hour. I had to stop looking at my watch because every passing minute sent me deeper into self-loathing. I despised being a source of torment to her. This was exactly the kind of power I didn't want to have over her. I was the embodiment of all I feared I would be, and I had become this monster of my own doing, in my own complacency. Eventually, I could take no more. I packed up my things and in the noise I made doing so, the hawk was startled and fell to the ground. I froze. She scrambled her way up the ramp to her perch and stood still gazing at me. We both remained motionless for the next fifteen or twenty minutes. I experienced how the blink of an eye can be like a lifetime. She preened a bit and was finally calm. Satisfied, I then left to prepare her food.

When I returned with her mice she was in the same place. She stood like a loaded spring as I deliberately approached her, but she did not twitch a muscle. I gently reached up and placed one mouse on the perch beside her, bowed my head in absolute respect, and took two steps back. She looked at me. Then, as if taking a sigh of relief, she bent down and picked up the mouse. In a few rips, tears, and gulps it was gone. I stepped toward her with the second mouse and as quickly as I placed the mouse at her feet it disappeared. By the third mouse, she was willing to take the food from my glove. In almost two hours I had managed to find myself in the company of a dear friend once again. At the time, those two hours were some of the most excruciating and soul-wrenching minutes of my life. In retrospect, the forgiving nature of this gracious raptor is absolutely astonishing.

Needless to say, our tandem training sessions didn't move gracefully forward from that moment. The hawk and I were still prone to anxiousness around each other, which made for the occasional overstepping of bounds and fallback in trust. Sensing there was more I could do to help with the process, I brought my story to my teacher, Galena. She went on a shamanic journey on my behalf to speak with the young red-tail and see if the hawk wished for a healing. There were three messages that came through. First of all, parts of the hawk's soul did fragment off during the surprise outing, and Galena did a soul retrieval around the traumatic event. My teacher brought back the bird's right to trust, safety, and contentment in her circumstances, and her right to not be exploited.

The second piece of information had to do with how my emotions affected that situation. The hawk felt that she was in danger and saw that I also felt a sense of peril. With her fear confirmed she completely gave in to it. We were in a negative feedback loop, continually reinforcing each other's terror. She was afraid for her life and I was afraid for our souls. We were both flung into survival mode. My job as her caretaker was to avoid exposing her to some of my own emotions because she couldn't understand the context of them. I was worrying she'd lose part of her soul, but she, as an animal of the wild world with no tools to unlock the bizarre workings of the human mind, interpreted that to mean she may lose her life. Losing the right to trust and to feel safe in the world may be just as horrible as death, but it was my role to offer a place of trust and safety so she wouldn't lose those soul parts in the first place. I wanted to be a companion with whom she could always feel content. By empathizing with her fear I was only perpetuating it. Galena explained to me that I needed to journey on a ceremony to hide the fear, anxiety, and worry that made me unsuited for my work with the hawk.

Galena then continued on in the journey to see if there were any soul parts of mine that would like to come back and help me. A huge flock of red-tailed hawks came in and raced over Galena's head.

"They've got their eyes on something," she said as she noticed them moving towards a little girl who looked like a younger version of me. The girl was lying down with her head in the crook of her arm, crying. She couldn't see the hawks. They were aggressively diving at her, trying to get her attention, to get her out of what she was doing, to get her out of her pain. Galena walked up and shook the little girl's shoulder. The hawks dispersed, apparently relieved that finally someone had come to help.

"Why did you leave?" Galena asked.

"Because there's just too much pain in the world," the girl whimpered.

"If you came back, what gift would you bring?" Galena questioned.

"My right to find joy in a painful world. My right to my joy in all circumstances. This doesn't mean I have to always be joyful, but at least I can find joy," she answered clearly, looking up at the red-haired shaman.

Galena lovingly gazed back. "Would you like to come back now?"

"Yes," the girl replied.

Galena gathered up the soul part and delivered her to me.

The final message of the journey came from Galena's spirit hawk, who had assisted with the healing. She wanted me to know that she was glad to help with the healing and that it was important that I have a positive experience with this red-tail because "the hawks have much need of you."

My ego wanted to believe that if I was a gift to the hawks then surely I could offer the young red-tailed hawk security and comfort as I stood, but clearly this was not the case. I was, after all, new to the world of falconry, and I had much to learn about my place in it. I humbly accepted the fact that I hadn't yet "arrived." I was not yet able to channel universal love and peace in an upsetting situation. I was still sitting on the island, trying to have a meaningful experience in the face of sixty mile per hour winds and bone-chilling fog. Eventually, I always succumbed to the battering cold and retreated inside into a lulling sadness. At the time, it seemed a paradox that the best chance I had to thrive while exposed to the wind was to hide my fears.

I went on a shamanic journey to lower world via the roots of my tree to meet with Thalia. I explained to her that I was in search of a ceremony I could do before entering the red-tail's cage to work with her. Thalia guided me to a mockup of the barn where the hawk now lived. We walked into the hallway of the barn and the spirit harrier gave me the following instructions. I was to stand in the hallway with my glove on, state my intent to "hide the fears that are not well suited for my time with the hawk," and then whistle for Thalia. I paced through the steps she gave me and as soon as the whistle left my lips, Thalia came flying head-on at me from the north. She landed on my glove, twittering in her lovely voice. I showed her the stone I planned to use in the daily ceremony to hide the fearful pieces of myself. It was a quarter-sized, rough, round lava rock. She politely requested the stone. I handed it to her, thinking she would work it in her beak and then hand it back. Instead she swallowed it. "Oooops!" I thought to myself.

"What now?" I asked Thalia.

"Blow the anxiety you need to hide into my mouth, so it goes into my belly and then into the stone," she responded. I quickly saw how this was a metaphor for the ceremony she suggested I do everyday before entering the red-tail's mews. I acted out the physical routine of holding my small cloth pouch with the stone inside in my gloved left hand, and whistling for Thalia. She flew in and landed on my glove, gripping firmly with her talons. With three scoops of my fingers I took the pouch into my bare right hand. With the pouch open, I held my lips to its mouth and blew the fears in. While I blew the fears into the pouch I saw the opening of the pouch as Thalia's beak and the inside of the pouch as her stomach.

"Will I always know what the fear is about?" I asked the spirit harrier.

"Not all of the time," she responded. It made sense that I should focus more on my intention and the ritual than what I was putting aside.

Now that I had hidden the pieces of me that weren't well suited for my time with the red-tail, I decided to go and talk with the young hawk to ask her name. Thalia and I traveled to middle world to the hallway in the barn as it stands. Neither Thalia nor any of my other power animals would accompany me into the hawk's cage. I turned to open the door and entered alone. I knelt once inside the door and bowed my head to the hawk in respect. Then I approached the hawk and asked her name.

"Gretchen," she replied.

Since we did not yet know the gender of the bird, I knew I couldn't convince anyone to accept a feminine name. There *was much debate over her gender because by her weight she was either a large male or a small female. I scrambled to think of a name related to Gretchen that would be androgynous. Silly names like Hansel and Gretel came to mind until she finally relieved me of my hopeless internal banter.*

"Graccia," she offered.

Feeling like the name would be well received in either a feminine or masculine context, I became immediately fond of it. The only person I had known of by that name was Nelson Mandela's second wife. I asked, "What does your name mean?"

"Gracious one," the spirit harrier informed.

It fit perfectly. I was pleased. I thanked her for talking with me, exited her mews, drew the pieces back into my being from the stone in the pouch, and returned home.

According to Mary Summer Rain and Alex Greystone, stomach relates to fortitude, which is defined as the strength of mind that enables a person to encounter danger or bear pain or adversity with courage. The word "fortitude" comes from the same root word as "fortress." In this ceremony, the black stone was to hold my fears while the pouch would serve as a fortress to protect them. Thalia was offering her stomach as the metaphor to lend me the courage I needed to hold the red-tail through stressful situations.

I also had the assistance of antelope medicine for this ceremony. The black stone I had intuitively chosen for the work was a stone I had gathered off the plains of Wyoming after an antelope hunt I rode along for. I was a child at the time and this was my first visceral brush with death. Without any guidance from the adults around me, I collected a few stones off the ground near the site of the kill. I ached for the soul of the doe that gave her life and eulogized her by carrying these stones like precious jewels. At home I stored them in a cedar box with a special prayer for the doe.

Ted Andrews, author of *Animal Speak*, gives the following insight about antelope: "They have a thick hide, sometimes an inch thick, which helps protect them from the environment. . . . For anyone with an antelope totem, there may either be a need to insulate oneself or a need to come out of hiding. The pronghorn can show how best to work with your insulation and help you develop a new sense of timing in relation to it."

According to Native American legends recorded in *Medicine Cards* by Jaime Sams and David Carson as well as in *Animal Wisdom* by Jessica Dawn Palmer, antelope was the first to give her life to feed man. She also embodied the virtues of courage to start new endeavors and to be of quick, decisive action. So it seems that every time I hid my anxiousness about my work with Graccia, I was receiving a healing. My fear was going to a safe place and was merging with and being nurtured by the energy of decisive action and courage. Now I could see that it was not the act of hiding itself that was causing my inner conflict, but the unconscious way in which I was suppressing my emotions. Now that I had entered into a conscious way of working with my fear, I was able to be more of who I truly was.

The beautiful ceremony was the first of two gifts from Thalia that came in the weeks after Graccia's arrival, and it served better than I could have imagined. Graccia and I had a string of lovely days alone in her room together. We made steady progress as I decided what our next task was and she showed me what worked best for her. She went from tentatively accepting food from my glove to flying the twelve feet across her cage to my glove. I was elated. She was beside herself because I'd finally realized that her favorite food was quail. Like any red-tail mother, I cut the quail into little pieces. Like a fledgling in the nest, she cried and cried for me to hand her more bites. She would sit eagerly on my glove, literally drooling in anticipation of the rich meat. I managed to squeeze more and more pieces out of the same size of quail every day. About two weeks after Graccia's move to her new home, the education program director, Sandra, took her for a walk outside alone. This outing went much smoother than the first and Graccia, from all accounts, adapted very well to the change in scenery. On Sandra's advice, I began taking Graccia for walks on the property on a daily basis.

We had an absolutely wonderful time together. Sure, she would startle at the occasional noise or passerby, but she would quickly recover to the glove after flying off and settle back into begging for more food. This was typical behavior for an ambassador bird. After a scare, they return to their handler for a sense of security and comfort. Most days we stood at the edge of the woods, her on her favorite post and I at her side, watching songbirds for long pauses. She stared at them with the intent of a fierce hunter and I gazed onward with the purpose of a curious student. Neither of us could manage to stand still for too long, so our bird watching was interrupted by rigorous exercise sessions. She flew from various perches to my glove as if it was her sole purpose in life. Whenever she'd become weary or anxious of the outside world, I'd carry her back to the safety of her home. We passed the last warm days of summer in this way.

One afternoon before I went in to get Graccia from her mews I heard the incessant calling of two wild hawks overhead. I looked up and as they circled I could see their adult red-tail feathers soaking up the warm sunlight. As they cried "Eeee-yaw," my mind questioned, "What are you saying?"

The wind pulled them towards the east, or maybe they steered that way with a few fingerlike feathers. They circled over the vacant field next door, one calling, the other responding. I could clearly make out the dark markings across their cream-colored bellies and wings. I don't remember seeing them flap but once or twice.

Then one of the birds tucked her wings to her body and dove straight down into the field. A few seconds later the male followed suit. They disappeared into the waist-high grass. Time stopped. I paused on drawn breath.

The answer to my question came barreling upwards with her parents in strong pursuit. The immature red-tail used her immense wings to climb straight up. Her stark white and dark brown belly flashed before me. The young bird had apparently been lingering on the ground too long. The family took flight together and set to soaring and talking in safety overhead. Eventually the thermals of the warm autumn afternoon carried them eastward towards the place of dawn and new beginnings. They moved upward out of sight.

When I entered Graccia's mews, I decided to offer her an invitation. I quietly approached her and placed my glove in front of her. With a simple "step up" from my lips, Graccia assertively placed both feet onto my glove. This was the first time she stepped onto my glove and went out for a walk without food. Of her own free will, she had chosen to join into partnership with me. We had found joy in all circumstances.

Sharing Joy

At the end of October when the rains and gloom of fall were upon us I stood in the clinic kitchen, preparing Graccia's meal. I heard a faint meowing from outside. Among the many creature voices at a wildlife rehabilitation center, this one was unheard. Wildlife rehabbers, as a rule, despise outdoor cats. Willow Brook admitted hundreds of wild animals a year, particularly birds and rabbits, that perished from bacterial infections as a direct result of cat bites or scratches. When a cat ventured to step onto the property, she usually heeded the general sentiment at the center and remained unseen.

I could only take about five minutes of the incessant whining from underneath the kitchen window before I opened the back door and wandered out into the mist to discover the source. The clinic was actually a mobile home trailer turned into a medical center, and one of the panels that closed off the space underneath the trailer had fallen off. I followed the meowing to the hole below and found a skinny black cat timidly staring out at me. Her coat was as black as the great void and her yellow eyes were bright enough to pierce any darkness. She crouched and meowed and begged. I saw that someone had put a blanket and bowls of food and water in her makeshift home. I didn't understand how she could still be so upset. I figured she'd either been abandoned or lost. I knelt down and gently reached to pet her. She met my hand and burst into a melody of purring. My heart was instantly enthralled.

I caught myself and woke up. There was a hungry hawk anxiously awaiting my arrival. I rushed back inside to grab the food and wandered past the gorgeous black cat to enter the barn. I stood outside Graccia's door, held the pouch with the stone in my glove, closed my eyes, and whistled for Thalia the spirit harrier. I watched her stunning, round face approach me in my mind's eye. She landed on my glove. Her presence brought me great solace. I stated my intent to "hide the fear that is not well suited for time with Graccia."

Thalia looked at me and said, "There's nothing to hide today."

I looked at her at first, perplexed. She turned my ears to the meowing that traveled down the hallway from outside. If a hawk could smile, she did at that moment. My heart beamed. I understood. This was the second gift my beloved friend from the other side had for me.

It was not enough that Thalia sent me her power animal, the black panther, to work with me in spirit. Apparently, she felt I deserved the assistance of an incarnate being.

I walked out of the raptor barn with Graccia on my glove to see the bold, talkative black cat meet eyes with the red-tail. The few moments they stood staring into each other's eyes inextricably linked their souls together. Neither broke their stare until I turned to walk off with Graccia.

Thalia knew that whatever grand scheme the black cat was part of surely aligned with mine. It was hard for me to spend only an hour or so of my day with Graccia. I wanted to bring the feeling I had with her into my life outside the wildlife center. I wanted the gift of the moment to permeate all aspects of my day.

For a number of months before I met the black cat, I actually had an unexplained yearning to bring a cat into our family. I had adopted a newfound fascination with the beasts. As a child, I was hopelessly allergic to cats, so much so that I couldn't even visit the houses of cat owners. But now, somehow, I knew that my affliction was healed and it was time.

I asked my husband, Chris, to join me on a trip out to the wildlife center to meet the cat and hopefully help me bring her home. We made our way through the pitch black, rainy night down the path to the clinic. He couldn't really get a good look or feel for her because she blended into the darkness so flawlessly, so I brought her inside. She proceeded to wander around the clinic crying. Chris could see that I was already in love with the cat and, although he didn't find her particularly charming as she yowled aimlessly, he agreed to bring her home.

We tried to shove her in a kennel, but she fought us, fiercely pushing against the kennel and squirming. Eventually, Chris picked her up, tucked her into his coat, and carried her home that way. It took a day or two for our yellow lab, Buckwheat, to accept her, but he too saw my love for the cat and acquiesced to the inevitable. As we took her into our family and brought her back to full health she returned the favor two-fold.

I had a companion in my home that shared a slice of this new world I was entering. She came as a gift from my dear friend Thalia and had been face to face with my beloved sister Graccia. Every time I buried my fingers in the feline's black fur or glimpsed into her moonlit eyes, I was linking back up with the wild ones. For this reason, I decided to name her after of one of the hawks. We called her Gretchen. By day my companion would be a hawk, and by night a black cat.

Receiving the black cat from Thalia reminded me of a valuable service I had to offer Graccia. It was time for me to retrieve a power animal for her. Life in captivity has its host of hazards, and extra protection and guidance couldn't hurt. I went on a shamanic journey to retrieve a power animal for Graccia.

I was led to lower world, where I joined hands with many if not all of my power animals and helping spirits as we stood in a circle. I stated my purpose, "I'm here on behalf of my friend Graccia to retrieve a power animal that would like to come back and help her, if that is in her best interest at this time." I stood waiting and watching for a power animal to present him or herself in the middle of the circle. At first I saw a porcupine. I asked the porcupine to present himself two more times if he wanted to come back and help Graccia. Next I saw a beaver. The first image that appeared to me was of the beaver felling a tree. The second was of the beaver swimming into the underwater entrance of his lodge. Last, I saw the surface of a pond in the last light of day. The beaver swam up and smacked his tail on the water. I invited the beaver into my arms and carried him through the roots of my tree to middle world and to Graccia's mews. She was a bit nervous when I first walked in, so I asked for the assistance of one of my helping spirits. He arrived and explained to Graccia that I had come to bring her a power animal. She roused and settled into her feathers. He asked her if I could blow the animal into her body. She agreed and walked down her ramp to a level where I could lean down and blow the beaver into her head. I then knelt beside her and blew the beaver into her heart with three more breaths. I thanked Graccia for participating and returned home.

Graccia was in like company with the tribe of the beavers. What first came to mind after I retrieved the beaver as a power animal was the busyness always associated with this waterborne totem. Graccia, like any beaver with a lodge to build and tend, preferred to "do" more than to sit. She was always interested in tackling a new challenge or working towards perfection of an old task. She also shared a primary physical characteristic of the beaver's: that paddle-like tail. She was famous for scuttling her tail like a rudder every time I put her on a perch.

Jamie Sams and David Carson, authors of *Medicine Cards*, summarize the medicine of beaver in this way: "Beaver . . . Teach me to build my dreams, Including others too. One mind, One thought, Hearts as one, Lessons learned from you."

The message of beaver gained more and more meaning as my relationship with Graccia grew. To my absolute joy, many lifelong yearnings of mine were fulfilled once Graccia and I started working together. I created my own job as an office manager at the local organic farm and had the long-awaited privilege of producing artwork for money. I designed all of their advertising and had free rein to create whatever made my heart happy. I'd dreamt of being a professional artist since my fingers first wrapped around a crayon. Now here I was, living my vision.

During my childhood I struggled with terrible hay fever and allergies. One of my strongest aversions was to hay. I adored horses as a little girl but couldn't step foot into a pasture or stable without breaking into dreadful sneezing fits and paralyzing sinus headaches. Within months of befriending this amazing hawk, I was riding horses twice a week without protest from my sinuses. I spent hours grooming the dust out of horse coats and seldom felt a tickle in my nose. I was also allergic to cat dander in my youth, but now I buried my nose in soft cat fur every chance I got. This hawk and I had clearly entered into a relationship overflowing with miraculous healing power.

In the months following Graccia's arrival, my personal aspirations came to fruition and I worked diligently to fulfill one of my primary wishes for the charming redtail. Before I even met the first ambassador bird candidate I knew that any raptor I trained had to be able to work with other people. After what I went through with Thalia, it was clear to me that a bird bound in captivity for life needed to readily accept new handlers. Education raptors who couldn't often faced an early death. I wanted Graccia to develop a sense of self confidence that would keep her comfortable on anyone's glove so she could live a full life. Realistically, I couldn't be there to work with her seven days a week, and she deserved to get out of her eight-by-twelve-foot room for at least thirty minutes each day. It was the least we could do to repay her for her life of service. Since most education presentations were during weekdays, I could only occasionally attend. As part of Graccia's role at the wildlife center, she was called to go to a dozen a year. Other handlers needed to be able to easily transport her to a novel location and work with her in front of a crowd.

In addition to wanting help with Graccia's day-to-day care, there was also the question of her long-term care. As many of my dreams started coming true, I started dreaming bigger. In the back of my mind I was working a plan to move out of state and attend a shamanic arts school in a year. I could not bring Graccia with me. She legally belonged to the wildlife center. For better or worse, this was her home, and I owed it to her to leave her in the care of others who she trusted. Here began the trying paradox of the times. To fully walk the path of my calling I was now looking at leaving the friend that helped me bring my gifts into the world. To make it through this dilemma, we needed helping hands.

Sandra Cuyler, the education program director, had developed a steady relationship with Graccia and was pleased with her progress. Unfortunately, Sandra left for four to six months every summer to be a river guide, and Graccia's second summer was fast approaching. I put out the call for help, and Eva Potter answered. A precocious young woman, Eva was outgoing and tractable. I liked her almost immediately. We had a lot in common. On the surface we were both short-statured women with no qualms about rolling up our sleeves and getting dirty. Deeper down, we balanced a reverence for nature with a child-like enthusiasm. Eva's enthusiasm was unabashed. I could tell this woman got a chance to play and giggle a lot more than I did. I was excited to get to know her better.

Until this point, Eva was primarily an owl gal. She carried a deep admiration of the wildlife center's great horned owl, Tskili, and spent hours resting under the canopy of the old trees on the property with him. They'd lapse into a quiet meditative state and she'd finally wander home once night fell. Eva had also started working with Papa Rhett and we quickly found that we had a shared adoration of the chatty owl. It was also no coincidence, I'm sure, that Eva grew up in the same town both of my parents did—Beaver Dam, Wisconsin. Eva was full of energy and good heart. A busy red-tailed hawk seemed a perfect balance to Eva's beloved contemplative owl. She was excited to join me in training and caring for Graccia.

In the early part of the year, Eva had worked with Graccia a day or two here and there when neither Sandra nor I could make it out to the center. She respectfully followed my instructions and diligently worked to earn Graccia's trust. To start, Eva and Graccia only worked together inside the mews. Like I did, Eva learned how many pieces she could squeeze out of a quail and took instant joy out of the red-tail's eagerness to fly across the cage to the glove. As I thought would happen, the two became instant friends. Eva was as busy a beaver and often had Graccia fly to her glove up to fifty times in a given session. I was astounded at Eva's willingness to spend so much time tediously walking from one end of the raptor barn room to another. They lived every moment they had together to the fullest.

As part of her fresh interest in the red-tailed hawk, Eva spent just as much time working with Graccia as she did watching me work with the hawk. She wandered with Graccia and I out to the small pasture adjacent to the raptor barn or out to the corridor lawn. As I asked the hawk to come to my glove over and over, Eva sat in the grass, cross-legged, and provided endless good conversation.

It didn't take long for either of us to notice that we had a shared interest in other worlds. We'd tell each other of the dreams we had the night before, or a peculiar way one of our feathered friends brought a clever insight. As my trust in her strengthened, I began to relate my experience with shamanic journeying, and she developed a quick curiosity in my studies. Through our shared love for Graccia, I was learning a new way to release my wild spirit, to have the courage to bring my gifts into the world, and to walk the path of my dreams. The conversations I had with Eva helped me open up more around other friends, and soon I was able to connect with a small soul family of women both at my work and at the horse stable. Soon it became plainly evident that my friends, like myself, were in desperate need of a place to voice experiences and feelings that didn't fit in the box of modern society. I followed the prompting these friendships fostered and arranged a gathering at my house.

A couple weeks before our meeting, Caruso, the lovely chestnut Arabian horse I was leasing, tripped and fell while I was riding him. I ejected from the saddle, and my hips and tailbone were badly bruised. I missed two days of work because I couldn't sit with the pain for more than an hour. I feared I wouldn't be able to ride horseback again for months and struggled dreadfully with the sorrow of losing the joy I'd just attained. I couldn't seem to think through anything, so I started acting on premonitions sent in my dreams. I went to the doctor with no hope of a diagnosis or cure, but because I'd been there the night before in my sleep.

Poking out from under the door of the nurse's office were the red and white stripped legs and black shoes of the wicked witch from the *Wizard of Oz*. *What bizarre décor to have in a doctor's office. It's not even close to Halloween*, I thought to myself, but at the same time it seemed to make perfect sense. Metaphors from the *Wizard of Oz* had been prolific in my journeys of late. I did seem like a tornado was at work in my life and it had just started to tear through town.

Five days before the meeting with my friends, to my complete shock and horror I came home to a full-blown construction site. My house sat on blocks with a three-foot trench dug around all sides. Parts of the foundation had already been jack-hammered away. There was a huge mound of dirt circling our home and the yard was littered with tools, supplies, trailers, and wood. I had left that morning to a quiet neighborhood, my house fully intact, with no warning that this was coming. The owners of the house we were renting had decided that three quarters of the house's foundation should be torn out and replaced. I had no phone for twenty-four hours and no rest for days. The workers would come at 7 a.m., turn on their stereo, and start slamming away at the foundation underneath our bed where we slept. The noise upset our dog so much that I had to take him to work. Everything was thrown on its head.

Clearly, to create a sincere environment to house my new soul family, I needed to tear down my outdated foundation. All the beliefs I held true and dear in the world needed to go. I couldn't guide a group into other worlds if I was fearfully holding on to this one. This message was coming through so plainly that it was manifesting everywhere I turned—physically, emotionally, mentally, and spiritually.

My soul sister was also showing me how to release my roots. Graccia had moulted (shed) two of her old tail feathers in the center of her tail. By the time the three women I'd invited made it to my doorstep, I was down to bedrock. I had no idea what to expect and with no ground to stand on I placed my fate entirely in Spirit's hands.

Like the beaver felling the tree, we began construction on the dam that would serve as the base of our new lodge. We gathered in my living room around a small candle on the wool sun deity blanket I'd spread out. My old yellow lab plopped down in the middle of the group, lavishing in lengthy belly rubs and occasional hugs. His fur collected in handfuls on the dark wool blanket. Everyone remarked on how soft his coat was and settled into comfortable conversation. We talked about the simplicities of the day and each woman, not knowing the other, settled into fresh relationships. Among the four of us we covered over twenty years, but in this room we regarded each other on level ground. My black cat Gretchen joined us, sauntering in from the bedroom on her long legs. She stretched out on the sofa overlooking the circle.

I began the evening by inviting each woman to talk about a place of honoring, meditation, or contemplation she may already have set up in her home. Quickly we learned that each one of us had, even if by happenstance, assembled an altar—a sacred space—in our homes. It was good to give voice to these places and to honor them in the circle. These spaces were quiet manifestations of our inner knowing, physical representations of life outside the mundane. Each woman spoke lovingly of these places and the support they'd received while being there.

I had a new set of animal cards that I unwrapped as we talked. I'm typically very superstitious with these decks of cards. The first card I see by mistake or on purpose is always the one I go with. While unwrapping the deck I carelessly turned it over and caught a glimpse of the bottom card. It was horse. This was perfect. I had journeyed the night before for instruction on how to advise my friends. One piece of guidance was to suggest each woman call in a horse to accompany her on her journey.

I pulled the card from the deck, and before I could lay it in the center of the circle, one friend, then the next, asked to see the picture on the card. As the card passed hands around the circle, we each shared about our relationship with horses. The room was split right down the middle between those who loved and those who wrote off horses. It was refreshing to hear the varied perspectives because in the mosaic of stories sat each woman in her truth. One friend asked me to give instructions on how to go on a shamanic journey. I hesitantly entered into lecture. These were my colleagues and mentors, and I found it hard to take a position of authority in the group. I quickly realized that I had information to offer that they couldn't find many other places, and my friends valued it as much as I did.

I started by explaining the basic shamanic perspective of the cosmos. "There are generally believed to be three worlds," I described, "lower world, middle world, and upper world. Lower world is generally of the earth and tangibles. Middle world is where we currently sit but free of time and space. Upper world is commonly of the ethers and subtleties." We talked about power animals and helping spirits. I gave them a series of phrases to clarify the idea of helping spirits—"ancestors, angels, spirit guides, and archetypes."

Each woman shared that she was already in a relationship with a power animal or helping spirit. None of them had visited a shaman or done a traditional shamanic journey. My friends had found their own ways to connect with Spirit. These women had vivid imaginations, which I explained was the key to the shamanic journey. They had already been journeying in their daytime and nighttime dreams, and it was my job to teach them how to visit these spirits and places intentionally. I gave them the ground rules for safety, explained how to travel to these other worlds, and instructed them to ask their guides for help. "I will drum for about ten to fifteen minutes," I told them, "and then I will give the callback beat, which sounds like this." I played seven beats in three sets followed by a fast rumble beat, and ended with seven more beats in three sets. They all lay down, one around my yellow lab, another on the yellow lab's bed, and another in between. I dimmed the lights and began playing my drum.

I was immediately enraptured by the sounds that rose out of each beat. The drum filled the room with twenty tones and moved the floor beneath us. Looking back, I jokingly feel fortunate that the vibrations didn't send the house off the blocks. In all honesty, I did not play that drum. She played me for the twelve or so minutes my arm could keep up. All the hesitancy, fear, and anxiety I felt over holding a group of such high caliber was completely overwhelmed by the music of the beats. Whenever I'd start to get self-conscious, my drum would pull me right out or in, depending on where I needed to be.

Before befriending horses, people could only travel so far. Through the beat of my drum, our allegorical horse, my friends and I traveled into other worlds. We had experiences that spoke of light, letting go, finding balance, and moving forward. The metaphors in their journeys wove a natural web through the circle. Two saw a yellow light in the northwest. Another pair had the experience of being hollow and full, being split between left and right, being heavy and weightless. Three of us never made it onto our horse's backs. We were all bewildered to one degree or another over our journey experiences, but the compassion we extended into the circle held us all in a good way. It was no coincidence that on my journey that night I followed a spirit red-tailed hawk into another world. The magic Graccia brought into my life was apparently at work again.

Spring gradually warmed into summer and many months passed before I realized that I had neglected to give Eva the go-ahead to start taking Graccia for walks. Eva was so content with whatever time she got with Graccia that she never expressed a want for more. The day after the summer solstice, I asked Eva to take Graccia out of her mews for a stroll. Graccia gladly accepted Eva's invitation to join her. No bribes were needed. I stood motionless in the hallway of the raptor barn and watched Eva carry Graccia to the back counter where the scale sat. I gave a few bits of advice as Eva carefully put Graccia on the scale to weigh her. The hawk sat calmly while Eva read "995 grams" out loud to me. Then Eva turned and looked at me, worried. She had forgotten to fasten the plastic sandwich bag of quail meat onto the waist of her pants. This was one of those things about Eva that made me chuckle. Many of us put the food in a hip pouch or pocket or bowl, but Eva preferred to use clothesline pins to hang the plastic bag of food from the waist of her pants.

She asked me if I thought Graccia would stand still and wait for her to fasten the bag to her jeans. I figured it was a long shot, but gave Eva the go-ahead. Sure enough, with all of the movement in front of her and being cornered in the narrow hallway, Graccia spooked. She jumped off the perch, onto the counter, and then down to the floor. She came running down the hall towards the door and past me. Instinctually, I reached down and scooped the hawk onto my glove. Graccia easily settled onto my glove with little concern. Flustered, Eva and I looked at each other and burst out laughing.

"Did you see her just chucking down the hall?"

"That was so cute how she just took off running. Where did she think she was going?"

Graccia's run down the hallway led us into a healthy gaiety that released our self-consciousness and opened us for new experiences. I had been holding my breath with worry, hoping everything would go smoothly for the two of them. Eva appeared rigid and scared, wanting to do everything right by both Graccia and I. We were like young beavers that eventually must leave the safety of the lodge for the outside world. For a few moments the young ones must hold their breaths and trust. When they make it out from underneath the dam to the water's surface, all they have to do is open their eyes and breathe in.

As I walked down the path beside the two of them that afternoon, I had the immense pleasure of being able to watch my dear companions bask in each other's splendor. Eva carried a natural awareness of the female hawk's movements and body posture. When Graccia would stir or shift, Eva would stop, take a breath, and settle into her own skin. Graccia would turn to meet her eyes and any apprehension would melt away. In this fashion, the two of them moved layer by layer into communion with one another. They carried a keen body awareness that spread beyond their own field and contentedly overlapped with the other's. Graccia knew Eva was going to hand her food before Eva reached for it. Eva knew Graccia wanted to face out of the sun before the sun hit her eyes. They spotted songbirds moving in the brush in unison. Their eyes darted to focus on a cottontail rabbit in the same instance.

All I had been experiencing on my own up to this point wasn't an illusion. I could stand aside and watch it move with my own two eyes. I could see Spirit stir in them as it did through me.

Eva and I giggled as Graccia's drool dripped off the tip of her beak. When Graccia took to crying for food and leaning off the glove towards the sandwich bag on Eva's hip we laughed harder. There wasn't enough quail in the world to repay this red-tail for the gift she was to us.

Soon thereafter the DNA test results on Graccia's blood came back from the lab. We found out that she was indeed a female. This affirmation of what we already believed to be true caused me to think back about the first name I'd chosen for her, Isabeau. Graccia was irrefutably the realization of my childhood dreams. However, she proved to be radically more. She was a messenger of Spirit in the true sense of the word. Her presence in the world, like a beaver's tail on a pond, sent ripples of gratitude outward.

⌒ 10 ⌒

On Healing Wounds

By this time there were two storylines running through my life. One storyline was made of fairy dust, granted wishes, and living dreams. The second was made of rising conflict, pending sorrow, and grueling tests. I had decided to follow my dreams and join the shamanic arts school at the beginning of the next year. My excitement and sense of soul purpose overflowed in my being. The horizon I approached was as brilliant as the one I parted. My time with Graccia was just as mixed.

Raptors in captivity are prone to mysterious sores and maladies. Papa Rhett, for example, bruised the base of his beak during the mating season of the wild great horned owls. We figured that the resident nesting pair was harassing him at night and that he was flying into the walls of his cage as he tried to get away from them, but we never really knew what was going on. All we could do was move him to a different mews and wait for his bruised beak to heal.

The entire time I knew the barn owl he had a crooked toe. No one could say when or how it was broken. These birds spend the majority of their lives in cages. Their bodies are meant for flying and instead we ask them to stand waiting. When a raptor is disabled they are even more prone to problems. Despite all the hours of exercise we asked Graccia to do, the droop in her wing didn't improve. This meant she was placing weight on her feet irregularly as she walked on her perches and that her right wing would get in her way from time to time.

In the early part of the year she developed sores on the undersides of two of the toes on her right foot. She was landing harder on that foot because she didn't have full use of her right wing to soften her landings. Foot sores on birds must be taken very seriously because without prompt and regular treatment they can lead to infections that can lead to amputation or worse. I was beside myself, of course, and tried to ignore the sense of doom looming in the back of my mind. I also did my best to disregard the worried looks on Sandra and Ian's faces when they found out.

I moved into action and immediately set to changing Graccia's living situation. Since she was using the same perches over and over, she was hitting the same pressure points on her foot continuously. One thing I could do to relieve this problem was wrap some new perches with rope and matting and set her up in a new mews. This way she would immediately start placing weight on her feet differently.

Once that was finished I had to face the dreadful task of caring for the sores on Graccia's feet. Of all my experiences as a vet tech, caring for animal wounds was absolutely miserable for me. As I lifted bandages I would cringe at open flesh and torn muscles. When I cleaned and treated wounds I tried hard not to twinge with each stab of pain the animal felt. Feelings of intense misery and fear of death would course through me. It often took all the strength I had to hold firm and provide a source of grounding to an ailing animal.

Ian suggested using tincture of benzoin on Graccia's foot sores. In humans this remedy is typically used for canker sores, but Ian had met some falconers who swore by its benefits for raptor feet. He told me that the tincture would work to toughen the skin on her feet and prevent further sores.

It turned out that the tincture served many purposes. It was incredibly sticky and would cover the sores for a couple of days, serving as a barrier to germs. The tincture was alcohol-based, so it worked as a keen disinfectant. The only trick was getting it onto Graccia's feet every couple of days. Luckily, I had a head start.

When Graccia first entered into the raptor education program, I started habituating her to my touch. I did this by softly laying the tips of my fingers on the tops of her toes. She would only tolerate a moment or two of this before moving her foot out from under my fingers and fussing. I would quietly move my hand away. It was important that I never flinch or startle when in such close contact with her. To do so could have meant talons stuck through my skin or losing the trust Graccia had afforded me. Every day I made a point of putting my skin in contact with hers. In a steady way we made progress to the point where she eventually didn't mind me laying my entire palm over her foot for extended periods. This also meant that she trusted me enough to allow me to pick up and manipulate her toes. This was a great exercise in confidence building. We both came to believe that one wouldn't harm the other.

The more captive raptors allow their handlers to examine them with touch, the safer they are. If a handler can freely examine and move the raptor's feet, she can regularly check for sores. This means that foot sores are caught early on before they become a serious problem. The handler can also trim the raptor's talons on the glove rather than having to wrap them in a towel and lay them down. This obviously reduces instances of stress for the bird. Feet are also a convenient place to loosely monitor a bird's temperature. Should the raptor appear sick or depressed, a touch of the feet may give some indication whether the bird is running a fever. Raptor trainers also like to be able to feel a bird's keel, otherwise known as their breastbone. This is another good place to get a hint of the bird's body temperature, and an even better place to check the bird's body mass and condition. I found that Graccia easily accepted my fingers along her keel once she was accustomed to me working with her feet.

All of this groundwork was complete by the time Graccia's foot sores appeared, so I hoped she would be relatively nonchalant about me applying the tincture to her feet. Some birds I knew, a grumpy barn owl in particular, would have had none of this. So it was hard to predict what would happen.

The tincture came in a brown glass bottle with a small mouth. The bottle didn't come with an applicator, so I visited the medicine cabinets in the clinic and stocked up on cotton swabs. The pouch I carried on my hip typically held a sandwich bag of Graccia's daily meal, a leash or two, a hand cloth, and some small hardware. Now I had a collection of cotton swabs and a bottle of tincture shoved in there too. This didn't sound like much until I had to manage it all with one hand.

First I had to sort through the pouch to pull out Graccia's leash and swivel to leash her up and get her out. Then I weighed her and walked her outside. She wanted a bite of meat fairly quickly, so I dug in my pouch around everything else to pinch out a morsel. She settled in as I walked her down the path to a waist-high platform. I fished out the bottle and a few cotton swabs and set them out on the platform. The liquid remedy was really sticky, which made the lid hard to pry off with both hands. With only one hand to do so, I was critically challenged. Graccia stood with a puzzled look in her eye as she watched me bite my lip and contort my right arm around the bottle. I laughed at myself with relief when the lid finally twisted loose.

The first time I lifted a white stick tipped with brown goo to her feet, she was unfazed and even curious. She turned her head sideways and bent down, saying, "What's that?" with her body language. Instead of acting like I was tearing her leg off, she made a sort of comedy act out of the whole thing. Sure, she flinched when I rubbed or pressed on the sores, but she remedied the discomfort by casually moving her foot away from my hand. When I lifted my hand back up to treat another sore, she reached down and grabbed a hold of the cotton swab with her beak. I chuckled, let go of the cotton swab, and watched her stand there with it in her mouth. She got this ridiculous look on her face as if she forgot why she wanted it so badly. It reminded me of a puppy that finally wins a tug of war. The toy never looks so great when no one else wants it. In disgust, she dropped the cotton swab and I started all over with a new one.

Sometimes she bent down to nibble my fingers as I worked. The tickle of her beak on my skin made me giggle. I had no problem getting plenty of the tincture on each of her sores and had loads of entertainment in the process. Graccia had managed, once again, to offer humor as healing. With steady treatments over a course of a couple months the sores on her toes disappeared completely and my utter distaste for treating wounds vanished with them.

I barely had a moment to sigh of relief before the next calamity of Graccia's surfaced. Eva called me on the phone me one night in early April with a worried tone in her voice. She had just peeked in on Graccia to say hello and saw a bloody lesion on her right elbow. She got Ian to help, and the two of them grabbed Graccia and took her to the treatment room. According to Ian, it looked like an old scab that had been pulled off. Eva had a different impression and was very concerned. We had no idea where the sore had come from in the first place. Eva reported that it was tender and large. She and Ian cleaned up the lesion, applied ointment, and bandaged it.

I talked with both Ian and Sandra about Graccia's condition, and they held out little hope that the wound would heal. They told me these kinds of wounds on captive birds almost never mend. Over the years they'd seen seemingly harmless punctures turn into festering wounds wrought with infection. No amount of the utmost in care and treatment made the wounds dissipate. Eventually the captive raptors with open sores had to be put down. Some of these birds were favorites of Ian and Sandra's and the experiences had scarred their optimism. I patiently held out for another miracle.

At the exact same time Graccia's newest misfortune appeared I was at a critical juncture in my life. There were a series of options set before me regarding my summer employment plans. The foremost option was to work as a vet tech at Willow Brook again. Since that position was part-time I could also keep my office manager position part-time at the farm. I had taken on a lot of new responsibilities at the farm, and my role would only grow as the busy summer developed. To only be there part of the week meant that I would have to give up some of my job duties. The position as vet tech at the wildlife center was just as important. I'd worked really hard to get the job the previous summer and already invested a lot of myself into the place. I knew my way around and would enjoy the time with the animals. I knew that if I didn't show for the position I would be letting them down. During my quest to find peace with this dilemma I continuously deliberated, journeyed, dreamed, and journaled.

Recently, Galena had brought me my higher self in a soul retrieval session. It had never occurred to me before that my higher self would make an effort to contact me, let alone offer to join me. In Galena's teachings she spoke of how there are many higher versions of each of us. As we evolve we move into the next highest version. She explained to me that my higher self had come to help me through the crisis point of shedding my former self. It took me a few weeks to become comfortable with this odd idea. I journeyed to talk with my higher self hours before Eva called to tell me about the sore on Graccia's wing.

My conversation with my guides evolved form and covered many topics, but ended on my plans for the summer.

"Why do you want to work at Willow Brook?" one guide asked. I noticed that she chose this place of employment first and only.

I answered bluntly, even surprising myself. "The higher pay and addition to my resume are appealing."

"That's it?" she asked me. I nodded my head. Now I could see that I was considering the wildlife center out of logic rather than out of my true desire. This was a complete reversal from the summer before, when I threw caution to the wind in pursuit of the vet tech position. How could that longing have passed altogether? All I could do was follow my instincts. If the job no longer fit me I needed to act on that now and ask why later.

My imagination naturally began to wander into the pending situation. Say I did trust my heart and turn the position down. As I visualized telling my supervisors and friends, I panicked. I fought for breath. It felt like ripping off a chunk of myself. I got it. I was struggling desperately with my decision to leave because my soul had become badly enmeshed with the wildlife center. In my haste to become a wildlife rehabber, I had given part of myself to the cause. If I wanted to continue on my path this enmeshment had to be broken.

One lovely spring day, I sat on a sun bleached wooden bench under an old oak tree. I was at Willow Brook near the corridor lawn. I had been stopped in my tracks by a red-shouldered hawk who stood on a limb and cried and cried and cried. This was the first time in my life I had ever seen one of these birds and I couldn't believe the intimacy of the visit. He was speaking directly to me. There was a vital message here. Just under the layer of hawk speak a universal language drifted. I could barely make it out. For moments on end I sat listening like a foreigner staring gravely into a native's eyes as he spoke. The hawk glared back, unwavering, a bull making a challenge. What was he saying? Why was he so adamant? Would I ever get it? Then it came plain. When I heard it once I heard it over and over again: "I—will—not—let—you—go." With a sigh of exhaustion, I stood up. The hawk flew away. I was overwhelmed. It was all I could do to return to the ordinary world.

Enmeshment sounds messy because it is. Let's make no bones about it. People who act to save others often do so in a desperate attempt to save themselves. I was no exception. Sure, we'd all like to believe in altruism, the giving of oneself for no return, but there is little case for selflessness in the human world.

As a society, we don't know how to trust. Without trust we cannot surrender ourselves. Instead of walking into the desert and knowing that Spirit will lead us to water, we build cities around rivers and lakes. We suck all we can out of freshwater supplies to have green lawns, fill enormous swimming pools, and stay clean. We obsessively hoard water out of fear of lack. There is little trust remaining. Society's programming tells us to "Accumulate wealth, lock your doors, cover your bodies, buy insurance, look pretty, and don't talk to strangers."

Here was a perfect example of choosing fear above trust. During my early months at Willow Brook, I did everything I could to win the vet tech position in record time, rather than trusting that the role of wildlife rehabber would come to me if that were my path. I was working from a place of fear and worry. From the outside no one would have known any different because I appeared self-assured and directed. Ultimately, I was thirsty and desperate to secure a source of water. I couldn't find the encounters, acquaintances, and kindness that fulfilled me in the human world. In my experience, people were too wrapped up in their own drama to offer balanced friendship. Animals were straightforward. They expected honesty in return. That was where I felt safe. I believed that this was the place I needed to be to fill my being. I felt this so strongly that I willingly gave up part of my soul for a chance to quench my thirst at the pool. This is where the enmeshment began.

I wouldn't have been able to give up a piece of myself if there hadn't been a place for it to be consumed. The other end of this exchange was also in the realm of the shadows and fear. The people who had been running to the wildlife center for years were themselves desperate. The non-profit organization couldn't operate without the valuable service of skilled volunteers and employees. Funds were limited, so the precious few thousand dollars they spent on veterinary technicians each summer needed to stretch as far as possible. Their seasonal employees couldn't just see this as a nine-to-five job—it had to be their lives, or the money was poorly spent. If a person came along and willingly handed over part of her soul, they'd gladly take it. At the time it seemed a fair trade and my only option: a piece of myself for a position at the wildlife center.

No one really wants to look at these kind of ugly exchanges, myself included, but ignoring them only serves to suck us dangerously dry. This was what Graccia was showing me. Lurking in the shadows was a tender sore. If the skin didn't venture to advance across the open wound her life force would flow out through it.

I was aligning with Spirit and the message was to refuse the role of wildlife rehabber that had meant so much to me. My skin needed to advance across this opening and close off my enmeshment with this place. If I didn't clear up the contract written in the shadows, my life force would be drained through it. The task of clearing this agreement was inevitable because I was leaving the wildlife center at the end of the year. It just turned out that I was being called to do it earlier than I expected.

Soon after the discovery of Graccia's sore, I went on the following shamanic journey.

I traveled to lower world via the roots of my tree and was led by a doe to meet with my higher self at a circle in the woods. I asked my question: "What do I need to do to free myself of the enmeshment with Willow Brook?" The red-shouldered hawk flew in and landed on my glove.

"He will help you," my higher self replied and continued, "We will need to travel to middle world and bring the many hands to help."

"Where can I find my soul part?" I asked.

"In the bone yard, buried with all the others," she answered. I knew exactly where that was. It was the place where many animals had been buried and also the place I went with my feathered companions to find solitude and privacy.

"Will I be able to release my piece only or do I have to release all of them to get to mine?" I inquired.

"You will need to free all that's hidden there," she answered. I hesitated for a moment at her cryptic wording and then surrendered to the process.

I began calling countless power animals in. Cougar, panther, grizzly bear, polar bear, mouse, red-tailed hawk, great horned owl, and more came to my side. Two mammoths and a cave lion joined us.

"We will need to disguise ourselves," she said. "You turn into a skeleton, like your picture of mother death, and I will appear like a ghost. That way we will go unrecognized."

We traveled through the layers of the earth, burrowing our way upward. We surfaced at my house and journeyed from there to Willow Brook. My higher self followed in my footsteps.

When we got to the bone yard and place of hidden soul parts we all began to dig feverishly. Even the mouse used his little paws to shovel dirt aside. I dug while glancing over at everyone who was pitching in. The mammoths were like bulldozers clearing the land. We all dug and dug. A turkey vulture kicked stubbornly at the ground. The big cats scratched away contentedly. The bears cleared paws full of soil at a time. Soon enough, we'd created a huge crater in the earth. At the bottom sat a palm-sized treasure chest. I crawled into the crater and gently picked up the small box. As the question began to form in my mind, one of my helping spirits arrived on horseback and stated, "the red-shouldered hawk will help you retrieve the spell you need to recite to open this box. You'll have to say the spell out loud three times." She left once her wisdom was departed.

The red-shouldered hawk came and lighted on my glove. I focused all my attention on the bird, gaining intense and bizarre views of his essence. I waited for the hawk to relay the message and followed the sound of the drum. The instant I heard the spell I spoke it. "I will let you go, you are not my foe." I focused my full intention upon the tiny chest in my palm. Energy surged through my being. "I will let you go; you are not my foe." The lid on the box began to crack open and an intense white light came blazing out. "I will let you go; you are not my foe." The chest flew open and hundreds, thousands, of lights burst free in a billowing cloud of colors. Some lights rained down into us. Tears fell from my eyes as I watched a light drop into my dear friend Thalia. As the lights fell, so did my soul piece into me. The golden eagle and great horned owls, Rhett and Tskili, Graccia, and Sped, all had a light fall into them. Some of the lights raced along the ground and away from this spot. Many of the lights shot upwards, disappearing into the heavens. It was the sum of all firework shows ever executed, then increased a full magnitude and expanded into a fourth dimension.

My scope couldn't begin to assimilate the meaning or magnitude of the event. It was unmistakable that I was a mere bystander in this healing process. I was both awestruck with gratitude and overwhelmed with humility. My life seemed a slight drama in the face of this spectacle.

I reached up to rub my eyes with my fists and come back into focus. Immediately the empty treasure chest came into view. It was resting on the ground. A mammoth took one leisurely step forward and squashed it under her foot. An army of ants and termites marched in to decompose the wood. As I watched the particles dissolve into the earth I said, "Let this wood be broken into its constituent parts and released to Spirit." I transformed back into my familiar form and the land healed itself, filling the crater back in and leaving a small scar. I returned home.

Over the next few weeks I watched Graccia's wing tenaciously heal itself, filling the open wound back in and leaving a small scar. I turned down the opportunity to work as a veterinary technician at Willow Brook and began my trek into the desert.

⤳ 11 ⤳

The Mouthpiece

Summer got off to a slower start than usual that year. At the beginning of June I stood in a field of knee-high crops photographing the cold dew hanging from angelic, white snap pea blossoms. The members of the community-supported agriculture program at the farm were ready for ripe red tomatoes, juicy strawberries, and crisp yellow summer squash. I had to explain why their boxes contained greens, greens, and more greens. I did my best to write a charming farm newsletter about the snap pea in the hopes I could persuade some members to be patient. The cool, wet weather was both a gift and a curse for us farmers. It gave our core crew, now in its second season together, a chance to prepare for the onslaught of summer customers. We were running a relatively new farmstand and café, and were just learning how to work together as an organism. Tensions would get high and sometimes the stress was unbearable. With only kale, lettuce, and endive to sell at the markets, the owners were anxious about profit loss. Greenhouses of spoiled potato seed didn't help matters either. Every day at work I was asked to help orchestrate and juggle a number of tricky projects. While doing so I also needed to learn how to relate to a group of vibrant and contrasting personalities.

As little as I knew of the intricacies of red-tail communication, I knew even less about human socialization. Interaction with people was something I had jumbled my way through on my way to the woods, the beach, and the island. I did my best to impress my parents, professors, and employers so that I could gain access to a world that made more sense to me. I entered into the field of ecology not because I always dreamt of being an esteemed scientist but because that seemed the best way to get to spend most of my time outdoors.

Now things were different. For the first time in my life, I was really challenged to interact with my own kind. I admired my co-workers at the farm and had faith in the work they were doing. There was a sense of family among them I hadn't found anywhere else. After an initial period of missteps, shifts in perspective, and generous acts, I was able to settle into my place at the farm.

Now for the first time in many years I didn't have a job working with animals. I had to find time to be with them on off hours. This meant that I got to play, relax, and be present with my feathered and furry friends. I began to focus less on what I needed to teach them and more what they had to teach me. The stable was on my way to work and I stopped in for a ride or some ground work about three times a week. I still spent four or five of days a week with Graccia as well.

One afternoon, I decided that it was time to offer Graccia the opportunity for companionship from another member of her species. She deserved the same sense of tribe that I was gaining. There was a young red-tailed hawk at the wildlife center that was recovering from an injury. Since the hawk had arrived at Willow Brook, the idea had lingered in my mind to pair Graccia with this newbie. At this time, the juvenile hawk was out in the sixty-by-thirty-foot flight cage well on the mend. She was a mellow bird who was quite tolerant of people. She had the fresh look of a young one that Graccia no longer carried. Graccia was now a mix of orange, cream, brown, and red feathers, while the younger hawk was purely brown and white. I had been given the opportunity to feed the young red-tail on a handful of occasions and I noticed there was a seriousness about this hawk. Unlike Graccia and her inquisitive looks, this bird stared back into my eyes solemnly. Regardless, I hadn't seen any signs of aggression in the new red-tail or Graccia so I felt it safe to at least give them a chance to meet.

I walked Graccia into the sixty-by-thirty cage. Graccia was firmly leashed to my glove and her attention was set on the pouch of food on my hip. The younger bird had her eyes fixed on us from the start. I talked with Graccia while quietly stepping one foot after the next towards the long beam perch the young hawk stood on. We covered about three quarters of the distance before Graccia lifted her head and spotted the other hawk. A few hackles on the back of her crown lifted. I offered her a piece of food. She let out a quiet cry and reached down to gently pick the morsel from my fingers. I knew both hawks would be safe if Graccia was more interested in the food than the new red-tail. As long as this was the case, I would be able to separate the two birds if there was trouble.

I took five more steps and arrived within six feet of the juvenile. She looked down at us from the high perch. I placed myself between her and Graccia. The juvenile stood frozen, watching. I handed Graccia another bite of meat. She swiped it quickly from my fingertips. Deliberately, I raised my arm and backed Graccia to the perch, maintaining a tight grip on her leash. She stepped onto the beam. Graccia turned to the juvenile and more hackles on her crown rose. She opened her wings a touch to make herself look bigger. The young one didn't flinch a feather.

Swiftly but gracefully, as not to startle the pair, I put food in my glove and asked Graccia to jump back on. She did so without pause. So far, so good. With the bite of meat settled into Graccia's crop I set her back on the perch. She took a few steps towards the young bird. The juvenile stood her ground. Again I asked Graccia to come to my glove for a piece of meat, and she did so without hesitation. She focused back in on me. I placed her back on the perch. Then her boldness got the best of her and she went sprinting across the perch towards the juvenile. As I was raising my glove full of food, she leapt at the belly of the juvenile, talons outstretched. The young bird stood her ground. Graccia's talons purposefully struck air. Graccia landed, I whistled, and she hit my glove, devouring the meat.

Graccia perched on my glove in her full glory. The entire crown on her head was lifted as well as the feathers on her shoulders and back. She looked like a massive crowned eagle straight off the plains of Africa. She held her wings outstretched in a magnificent cape and held her crushing beak open just ajar. There was no mistaking who was lead hawk. I was thoroughly awed. As for the juvenile red-tail, she was doing a fabulous job of standing stoic and appearing entirely unaffected by this ludicrously brilliant display. I noticed that I was beaming with pride while at the same time riddled with doubt.

Being a relatively skilled birder and naturalist, I knew that I was walking a thin line. Once animals decide they own a certain space they will often do whatever is necessary to make that clear. It seemed that Graccia was picking a fight she intended to win. I reminded myself that I didn't speak or live red-tailed hawk. This could be some average ritual they'd play out for a time without ever touching each other. For all I knew they could be shaking hands and saying "nice to meet you." On the other hand, they could be spitting nasty putdowns at each other. It wasn't my place to decide. Graccia had demonstrated that I, or at least the food I carried, was ultimately her bottom line. It was also evident that Graccia was only putting on a show. She could have buried her talons in the juvenile if she chose. I felt it was safe enough to stay here a bit longer and see how these two chose to become acquainted.

I handed Graccia another morsel of chick meat. She let out a sweet baby cry to ask for the food, picked it from my hand, gulped it down, and stood focused on me. I was completely enthralled. Here I stood in the company of a hawk dressed in full fighting regalia who was using baby calls to beg me for food. This was too much, and practically my favorite Graccia moment yet.

I asked her to step onto the perch and passed her another bite-sized piece of chick. She leaned down and took it, still intent on my habits. I took a deep breath and stepped back. Graccia awkwardly turned to face the juvenile. It didn't look easy to carry that big show around. I smiled and was once again surprised at the seriousness the juvenile held. That didn't look like an easy costume to carry either. Her worry seemed just barely tangible. I'm not sure she was breathing because she managed to stand so still. Then, with a hop, skip, and a jump, Graccia's talons were again headed at the belly of her counterpart. The exact same scene played. No feathers were ruffled and Graccia ended up securely perched on my glove. "Okay," I whispered out loud to Graccia, "you get one more chance to make nice and then we're done."

I placed her on the perch, and this time she didn't pause for a second. Graccia was across the beam before I could blink, lurching at the young hawk. The juvenile lost her ground and reeled backwards to avoid the conflict. She stumbled back and off the beam. Graccia stood victorious, towering above her opposition. If I thought she looked ridiculous before, now she was bordering on obscene. I ran up, swept Graccia onto my glove, and put some distance between us and the young bird. The juvenile stood on the ground, appearing both shocked and mad, but unharmed. Once I knew she was fine I strutted out of the cage with the trophy bird on my glove.

Eva met us outside. She had been getting an owl out for a walk and overheard me yelling at Graccia. I hadn't been able to stop my outburst as Graccia pushed the youngster off the perch.

"What was going on in there?" Eva wondered in a loud and worried voice. I never yelled at Graccia, and it was clear that Graccia had been through something. She continued to stand on my glove like a lion with this massive mane of feathers spread all around. I quickly recounted the story to Eva and then we lapsed into minutes of laughter. Graccia wasn't ready to shake the garb. We were standing and having this perfectly relaxing conversation and she looked like she was out to win the costume ball of the century. It was almost as if she was encouraged by our laughter. She carried on in her robes as if the gaudiest costume won the contest.

Graccia was to the point that she could easily perform all of the tasks there were to ask of her. This included getting in and out of her travel box as well as acclimating to new environments. It was time for me to take her to a presentation and get her career as an education bird underway.

As I was preparing all the equipment and supplies for the presentation, I was in a frantic and crabby mood. I knew Graccia's livelihood depended on this event going well. With the string of maladies Graccia was prone to, the wildlife center would only work to keep her healthy if she proved comfortable in front of groups. If she didn't do well at presentations, one more malady could be enough to convince the education crew that she wasn't meant for a life in captivity. My thoughts circled and my emotions simmered. It seemed so unfair that her life and value was measured in what she could do for a group of strangers.

I knew my mood wasn't going to help anything, though, so I paused for a moment to take a deep breath and clear my head. I asked myself what I wanted of the experience, what I wanted for Graccia and me. My response was, "for us to be in our truth, to be safe and secure, and for the space of our experience to be held." I stood in the sensation of this desire for a moment past the thought and set back to getting Graccia, Eva, and Tskili to the school where the program was scheduled.

Everything quickly turned chaotic and frantic again. We had bad directions and barely found the building where we needed to be. We had to walk all the way across the building with the large raptor travel boxes, trying to hold them as steady and quiet as possible. The group that hired us had double booked our slot so we had to stand for a half an hour and listen to a different talk. We were supposed to rendezvous with another education program volunteer and never found her. I scurried all over the building and grounds searching for her. Finally, I got up in front of the group and began our presentation. By this point I didn't care much to be there, but from the moment I opened the door to Graccia's carrier, saw her face, and had her step onto my glove, my whole experience shifted. The entire room dissolved. My anxiety melted away. The truth in that space was she and I. I was elated and she was amazing. She stood animated on my glove, crying for bits of food, and curiously surveying the crowd. Everyone appeared enraptured. I knew that we were safe. I felt us beam. We held the space purely by living our own truth.

This experience triggered a sizeable shift in my worldview. Holding space was no longer an ethereal idea, but rather a reality. Graccia was showing me how to stand in my truth in front of a group of absolute strangers. It was a profound and uplifting sensation. These twenty minutes in time set the stage for the majority of the shamanic work I've done since. This is what I had to learn to walk my path. Without the ability to hold space I would never be able to stand in the glaring spotlights of the human world. I was starting to understand that this was what the animals were asking of me. They were asking me to bring their vision, their viewpoint, on stage. I didn't really understand the gravity of this request until I looked into a troubling mirror one evening in late July.

I was at Willow Brook, waiting for Graccia's dinner to thaw. Zoe Gray, my former fellow vet tech, came through the front door with a tall cardboard box in her arms, exclaiming about a long drive to pick up an injured red-tail. I followed her into the exam room and she set the box up on the treatment table. Whoever had caught the bird had readied the box nicely. There were two-inch by two-inch inch square windows cut out all around the outside of the box. The people had reportedly found the hawk on the awning of their porch.

I crouched down to peer inside. The hawk's eyes bravely met mine. The light of her spirit pierced the shadows of the cardboard surrounding her. I remained motionless, entirely transfixed. I'm not even sure that I drew breath. Those eyes held so much light, so much life. She stood so strong and assured, but the whole picture was askew.

This hawk was missing at least half of her upper beak. There was no way to imagine how this bird had survived the pain of the injury and the subsequent bleedout. I was staring into the eyes of the impossible and couldn't find my feet. Her right wing hung low. I figured she must have injured that too. I heard Zoe's voice from across the clinic. She was tending to another animal. I decided I'd leave the hawk for her to care for since I was no longer on payroll and it was Graccia's mealtime. Graccia was waiting for me at her door.

The energy of the injured red-tailed hawk hovered with us during our entire outing. Everything seemed to carry such purpose. My love for Graccia was overpowering. Graccia took in the whole world around her with so much innocence. I enjoyed her company so completely that I lingered with her past my dinnertime. I eventually left Graccia in her mews and made my way back inside to write in her log book:

"17:30. Weight = 973 grams. Food = 1 chick and 4 mice (100 grams). Long walk outback. Time on glove. 20 jumps from A-frame perch. 45 minutes training time. Lovely outing! She was at the door. I oiled her jesses before jess-up. She waited patiently. No bates on walk to

A-frame. I fed her bits of food along the way. One rouse on A-frame. Only one bate on long walk way outback. Very interested in everything. Anxious on walk back up but no more bates. Lots of crying. Such a nice girl."

∽

The injured red-tail was still standing in the box on the treatment table. I called my husband to let him know I would be a while and turned to offer my services to Zoe. She gladly accepted my help. I grabbed a pair of thick gloves and a towel to gather the hawk out of the box. The hawk struggled and fought my grasp. I was astounded at how much strength she still had in her crippled body. We laid her on the table still wrapped in the towel, and pulled her right wing out to examine it. The bones were badly broken halfway between her elbow and wrist. All the tissue around the fracture was heavily swollen and damaged. We could see that the bones had healed at an odd angle. There was no way she could ever fly again. Her fate was sealed. As Zoe placed the isoflorene cup over the hawk's broken mouth, I ran my fingers along the bird's keel. There was no flesh there. The width of my fingers sunk into the feathers below the crest of the keel. All I could feel was bone. I looked up at Zoe and asked her to confirm my observation. She buried her fingers in the soft down of the bird's breast and then shook her head in disbelief.

"How is this bird still alive?" I said out loud. "How is it still conscious, still standing, still fighting my grip, still watching?"

This was the walking dead, a sacred omen. We were in the presence of a blessed beast. I was having an extraordinary, out of body experience. There was no way this bird could have been breathing, let alone matching my gaze or standing. Now she was in a sleep she would never wake from in this body again.

A while later, I went back out to the old barn to retrieve the red-tail's body. I brought it inside to put it in a bag and label it. A wildlife rehabilitation center often serves as a mortuary as often as a hospital. Still in shock, I stood inside, turning the body over and over in the palms of my hands as if somehow I could unlock the mystery like the twist of a key. I ran my fingers up and down the starkly bare keel. *There is more for me to see here*, I kept thinking to myself. I continued turning, continued passing my palms over the omen. Then I picked up the tail and spread out the feathers. Earlier Zoe had told me that this hawk was an adult bird because she'd caught a glimpse of red tail feathers. The center two tail feathers were red and fully grown. The feathers on each side of the center pair were red and halfway emerged. The rest of the tail feathers were brown. This bird was the same age as Graccia. In fact, it had the exact same moulting pattern on its tail as Graccia. This hawk also had a right wing injury markedly similar to Graccia's.

This omen did not bode well for Graccia's future, especially since her body was ailing for yet a third time. She was well into her first moult. Birds typically drop and re-grow their whole coat of feathers every year. Of course they don't drop them all at once, but in a gradual progression. In red-tailed hawks, tail feathers are moulted in pairs and each wing looses one flight feather at a time. The new feathers emerge as "pins" which are a keratin sheath full of nerves and blood that provide the nourishment needed to generate the feather. The pins grow to about three quarters of the eventual feather length, the feather at the tip of the pin emerges, and the live tissue begins to retreat towards the body. The keratin sheath then dries up and flakes off the feather. All of the feathers on Graccia's unimpaired body were coming in beautifully. It was the flight feathers on her right wing that were not following this natural process.

Graccia kept inadvertently knocking the pinfeathers on her wing against perches. She tried to hold her wing out of harm's way but her elbow was fused in an open position. There was little she could do. When these pinfeathers were bumped over and over they broke and exposed blood and nerve tissue. Luckily, her body was proficient at clotting, so she didn't bleed more than a few drops when each pin would break. The bad news was that the severed nerves caused pain. Days after the pinfeathers broke, they fell out, and new feathers started.

At first we hoped that she would only break a few pinfeathers, and that once a few feathers fully developed they would be able to act as splints for the subsequent feather growth. I kept a close eye on Graccia, taking studious notes and gauging her behavior in relation to the emerging feathers on her handicapped wing. While I was with her I never saw her pick at the pinfeathers or flinch when the wing bumped something. She was good at ignoring the pain, but we couldn't ask her to bear it indefinitely.

Once again I turned to Ian, Sandra, and Eva for counsel. We all agreed that if this painful malady proved cyclic that we could not ethically justify keeping Graccia in captivity. There would be no option but to end her life. I contacted experts in the field in hopes of finding a solution. Maybe there was a surgery or medication that could somehow interrupt a continual moult. No one could offer an answer. Regrettably, around the same time I encountered the foreboding omen of the walking dead hawk. It was becoming more and more plain that Graccia's wing had fallen into a permanent moult. She was on the second or third attempt at growing feathers in some follicles.

Passing the otherworldly, deceased red-tailed hawk through my hands brought a disheartening knowing fully into my being. Graccia's life could well be cut short by euthanasia. The choices ahead were far from easy, but at this point I could no longer ignore the dark cloud on the horizon.

One solemn mystery of the omen was solved, but I still hadn't figured out why the otherworldly hawk was missing most of its upper beak. I puzzled over this for a number of weeks. The full story had yet to be written. One afternoon, on a car ride out to our friends' farm on the Pacific coast, I had a chance to take a light nap. The hawk with the missing beak came to mind as our car wound through the lush green forest. In the place between sleep and waking, one word drifted in. One word explained it best. That hawk was missing her mouthpiece.

I took the first chance I got to go on journey. The opportunity came a couple mornings later. I borrowed a blanket and rattle, shouldered my drum bag, and walked down to my favorite grove of Douglas fir trees just past the chicken and duck coops on the property. As I broke into the forest, the canopy towered overhead, and I was drawn to one of the grandfather trees lit up by the morning sun. I sat down, crossed my legs, and faced the tree.

I journeyed to upper world via the grandfather tree and spent some time communing with a golden eagle and dark red dragon until I was prompted to return to middle world and journey to speak with Graccia. Thalia and the black panther were the only ones that came with me into Graccia's mews. My red-tailed companion told me she loved me and that I was the best friend she'd ever had. I felt the love radiate from my heart to match hers. We talked about her burial and where it was to be. She told me that where I chose to bury her would change the course of my life. Next I asked, "What can you tell me about the red-tail that mirrored you? Why didn't it have a mouthpiece?"

Graccia wouldn't answer my question and instead sent me to the mews next door to ask there. I'm sure it was no mistake that the neighboring mews was once Thalia's home. At this time in ordinary reality, there was a short-eared owl in recovery in the cage.

Once again this combination of northern harrier hawk and short-eared owl had resurfaced in my life. The spirits of the island perpetually found their way into my dreams, journeys, and everyday life. The harrier hawks seemed to do all they could to bring the fantastic to me while the short-eared owls did all they could to entice me to venture into other worlds myself. Maybe this time I would be able to make contact with one of the short-eared clan.

I opened the door to the mews and found the owl waiting to speak with me. I looked into the bizarre round mask with tribal markings and asked the same question I'd asked Graccia: "What can you tell me about the red-tailed hawk that mirrored Graccia, and why didn't it have a mouthpiece?"

The short-eared owl responded bluntly. "You are our mouthpiece. We have given all of our life energy in trying to communicate with you humans and we have no life left. We are the walking dead. We can no longer speak for ourselves. We are asking you to speak for us."

Of course this left me with the dying questions, "Why me?" and "How do I speak for you?" These questions were simply left unanswered.

Even though Graccia and I had talked so plainly about her burial, I had to I take our plans and set them aside. The final say in what would happen to her was not mine. The path to her fate rested in many hands. I had begun to come to terms with my own emotions and doubt, but not those of Graccia's other caretakers.

☞ 12 ☜

The Angel of Fiery Red Trees
and Golden Grasses

Graccia's fate was weighing more heavily on me as each day passed. I'd been in quite a state. I was in a dizzying cycle where for five minutes I'd live in full clarity and truth and then for the next five minutes I'd face images of myself distorted in a funhouse of mirrors. My vision of the world was blurred. I was thoroughly disoriented. Ultimately, I didn't know how to face the truth I knew: that soon I would have to let go of Graccia. So I sent myself into denial every five minutes to cope. It was easy to doubt my intuition because this was not a clear-cut case of terminal cancer or imminent organ failure. No wonder I was feeling nauseous. I called for a second gathering of friends at my house in hopes that the company and enfoldment would lend me some peace of mind. My three dear friends came and offered me the chance to rest surrounded by their companionship. Within the circle I felt grounded enough to attempt a healing journey for myself. My drum pulled my hand into her hide and her voice boomed into the room.

I followed my red dragon into lower world, where she led me to a raging volcano. We were in the midst of burning, erupting lava with the night sky as a backdrop. We pulled back from it a bit to take in the sight of the whole volcano. "This is your intuition," the dragon told me, "strong and intense. You need to spend the next five days or so sitting with a blue flame as an alternative because this fiery lava will be too destructive in your life." The blue flame was cool, precise, and calming to me. Then the dragon said something I almost carelessly dismissed. "Once Graccia has passed out of this world you will see her when the hawk covers the earth." The image of an enormous hawk wrapping her wings around the planet materialized before me. It was an awesome sight to see. It was also totally impossible. I found no hope that I would ever see this phenomenon in my lifetime. Hence, I believed there was little promise that I would see Graccia after she passed. In the end, that was reasonable. In one year of reverence I'd exchanged lifetimes worth of love and joy with this inexplicably gorgeous beast. I had no path but to hold an abyss of gratitude. I began to release myself to the process.

As I sat with the thought of handing Graccia over to the other side, my heart flooded with soothing bliss and meandering sorrow. There was no question now as to whether it would be my arms carrying her across. This was my sacred duty. I did not worry about how to perform a fitting ceremony for my mythic spirit guide. My friend had already shown me the way. All I grappled with was when. When would be the perfect time to pay homage to such a dear mentor? When would the stars be aligned and the gate swiftly open?

I knew it had to be a noted day on the calendar of seasons, just as Thalia left on the summer solstice. Summer was now waning and all my gravity-drawn mind could think of was the autumn equinox. That was over a month away and on a weekday. There was no way that both Eva and I would be able to get out of work. I was under the impression that others in the education program were getting anxious for me to carry through with the decision to euthanize the hawk. I emailed everyone to let them know I'd decided to go ahead with it, but I was still trying to buy time until the appropriate date became apparent.

Ian approached me in the last light of day as I stood with Graccia on my glove. "I don't like that you told everyone in the education program that you've decided to put Graccia down but that you plan to wait several weeks," he opened.

"I never meant to come across like I own her," I replied honestly, "I thought everyone had already given up hope for her and that they were just waiting for me to be okay with it."

Ian looked at me with a disdaining air. "Well, that makes sense, but I think we need to take a few steps back and have one more meeting to come to a formal decision together."

"That is no problem at all," I answered, relieved to share the responsibility. Graccia stood calmly on the fence post perch facing the space between Ian and I. Occasionally her attention would wander to a robin darting among the trees or a house finch nibbling on branches. Mostly she was present for the conversation. She may not have understood our words but she clearly responded to the gravity of the topic. The curiosity in her face was absent.

"Why do you need several weeks?" Ian asked.

I could not state the truth because I knew how ridiculous it would sound. In our society there is no perfect time to die because dying is inherently flawed. I feared Ian would see my search for synchronistic timing as a feeble attempt to avoid the inevitable. Sure I was scared, but my sense of duty to this hawk far outweighed any fragile emotion. I scrambled to find some honest but hazy response. "I need time to prepare her burial ceremony."

Ian shifted his weight from one foot to the other. "I could provide sufficient ceremony in a few minutes, but I understand that other people must do so in other ways in other time," he said in kindness. "But it would ease my conscience if you could keep in mind that we need to balance your need for a proper ceremony with Graccia's need to be released from this pain."

"Fair enough," I replied. "I want to be clear that if either Eva or I saw Graccia behaving like she couldn't bear the pain, we would not hesitate to end her suffering immediately."

"To be honest with you, I never thought Graccia would last very long. She's always seemed like a nervous bird to me and I never thought she would do well at presentations," Ian begrudgingly admitted.

My tongue held back the words: *I know you've been saying this to other people behind my back. Why did you wait a year to say something to me?*

Graccia was so calm still. If I was confrontational now, we would only prove him right. My emotional reaction would only solicit "nervous" behavior from her. I took a deep breath and stared into the hawk's eyes. She looked back, unwavering. I felt my frustration sink back into the earth via the soles of my feet. I turned to Ian. "I'm disappointed that you have thought that all along and never said anything to me."

"I'm sorry," he replied calmly. Then, as if waking up from a long sleep, he turned to look at Graccia. He blinked his eyes a few extra times to pull her into focus. She tilted her head sideways, reflecting his inspection as if to say, "What is it you see?"

Then he responded, "Well, now look at her. She's sat calmly the whole time, not fidgeting at all, not picking on her feathers or wing. She looks comfortable."

It had taken Graccia and I a year plus one half an hour, but we had finally prompted this man to see the truth of us. There was no agenda here. He had searched for hidden motives and found none. Graccia was my companion in the world rather than my escape from it. I promised Ian that I would ask the other volunteers of the education program to join me in forming the final decision about Graccia.

A week later, in the hour before the big meeting, Graccia met me at the door of her mews. She'd gotten in the habit of expecting me at a certain time of day and made sure she was the first thing I saw as I cracked open the door. It didn't matter how many times she would wrench her neck around to peek at me as the door opened—I would giggle every time. Instantly, my heart was open and she was my world.

We went to her favorite fencepost and relaxed quietly, side by side. I stood with my feet firmly anchored in the ground while gazing into her face. She stood, talons calmly resting on the carpeted perch. I had been riddled with worry all day in anticipation of meeting with the education program members. I expected that I'd have to answer to all of the nasty doubts that lurked in the back of my mind. *Had I kept her alive and in pain out of selfishness? Was I reacting too swiftly? Was there more I could do? Had I made the wrong choice by bringing her into the education program in the first place?* Countless times I had stood before my critics in tears, demoralized. I wasn't sure this wouldn't happen again. *Could I stand in my truth and trust what I had chosen up to this moment?*

I raised my eyes to look up at Graccia with the face of a mouse cornered in a maze. My front paws rested on the walls that confined me. I would have pathetically twitched my whiskers if I'd had a set. She looked back, as if to say, "What is it little mouse?"

I drew in a long, deep breath. My nervousness and apprehension began drifting into the earth. Graccia gazed intently into my eyes. "Hold on, little mouse. I'll get you out of there."

Instictively, I took a series of deep, cleansing breaths. Graccia reached out her wing and stretched her neck to one side. I rolled my ear towards one shoulder and then towards the other. The vertebra in my neck settled into place—"click, click, click,"—as my muscles extended. The disengaging of tissue was so satisfying. Graccia roused and settled into her coat of feathers. I methodically worked through each muscle group in my body, carefully stretching and releasing. Typically, the curious hawk would have found my body contortions amusing. On this evening she stood attentive. I noticed she had more red than brown tail feathers now. With each exhale and extension I was more sure of myself. The cloak of outside judgments lifted as a fog carried off by a quiet breeze. I felt the cool night air flow across my bare skin. Graccia's attention moved to a rabbit grazing nearby.

Oftentimes the rabbit is associated with fear in folklore. I seem to encounter them once I've moved through fear and followed my nose down a rabbit hole. Graccia was leading me into territory so fresh that I was unaware of what had happened. Like magic, I was myself, the anxiety lost. Like magic, she'd lifted me from the maze, the confusion forgotten. I'd released myself to the way of the hawk and was better for it.

After taking Graccia back to her mews, I made my way to the meeting place. Eva and I brought all the evidence we had to the table for the group to review so everyone had a chance to come to peace with the decision. They were all fair, compassionate, and supportive, each coming to terms with their own sadness over this difficult situation. In the end, the voice of my own inner critic was the only monster I had to face. That realization set me free. Now the debate was through and I could move on to honoring my dear friend and walking her across the veil.

I let go of my need to control the timing of her passing and agreed with the group that her last day should be in ten days, on Saturday, September 17th. On the Sunday preceding, I set aside an afternoon for Graccia. We went on a long walk past her favorite perch and the A-frame perch. We passed the raccoons and went over the last footbridge. There was but a trickle of water in the stream below. When we came into view of the bobcat youngsters in the predator pen, we stopped. These sister cats had been growing up at the very back of the property over the course of the summer. They'd come to the wildlife center via a logger who found the kits abandoned in an exposed den in a clear-cut.

I was curious to see what the girls were up to. They were pacing around their pen making all sorts of noise as we approached. Once they noticed us they paused, mulling over their next action. One of the cats wandered up to the chain link that stood between us. She stood up on her back legs to see over the short barrier of plastic that lined the walls of the cage. Casually, the sweet feline placed each large mitt of a front paw through a hole in the fencing. With her enormous paws protruding from her prison she stood calmly staring at us.

Graccia was a bit taken aback. She raised her hackles slightly. My plan was to take Graccia to the meadow, which meant we needed to navigate around the curious kittens, so I softly moved a few steps closer. Miss Graccia's feathers became more ruffled. I gathered a morsel of quail from my pouch and handed it to the hawk as if to say, "you are safe with me."

As she crouched down to devour the meat, she fluffed into full regalia, crown erect, wings held half out. This masquerade sufficiently hid her snack from view of the bobcats. Graccia's wariness gave me incentive to break from the stare of the standing bobcat and walk on past the cage. I could only escape from the inquisitiveness of the cats momentarily. When we got to the other side of the pen I couldn't help but look back. This time, both sisters came to the wall, and, in tandem, they stood up to push their paws through the chain link. Their big feet were one, two, three, four, all in a row. Their sweet faces looked out inquisitively at the woman and the hawk. I felt Graccia's weight shift on the glove. She was ready to move on. I turned towards the path to the open pasture.

We'd only been out to the far end of the property together once or twice before, so the experience felt like a new one to share. She sat patiently as I wound and wove through the tall brambles on the narrow path. I would first lift her over a bush or dip her under a limb before following myself. I sensed apprehension in her. She seemed unsure of what this adventure was all about, but stronger yet was the bond of trust between us. Graccia was most assured that all would be well with me there. My love for her was in the open and infinitely present. I felt so blessed to be with her and to watch her go out into the world, keenly confident with me by her side. How spectacular that I had been handed the care of this bird and that in this moment, as we tackled stray blackberry thorns and towering thistles, she was in her own. The red-tail was ever present, ever open, ever content. What a gift to know such a soul and be so intimately in relationship with this angel.

We traveled back to where the old trailer sat just inside the fenceline. A wild red-tailed hawk called nearby. I followed Graccia's line of sight to an old oak tree in the field to the east. The wild hawk lifted up with stunning flaps of long, strong wings. Then it flew to the north just out of view, only to fly back to its initial roost. It called again to a companion that was out of sight. A shrill cry answered from the northeast. The scene went on like this for a time, with the wild hawk flying north and back, and the two voices crying in conversation. We stood and watched and listened until our friend disappeared from view and the dialogue stopped.

I carried Graccia to the west, towards a gate, through thistles mostly taller than myself. I lifted her up and above and down and around the dry seed heads, picking my way forward. She concentrated on maintaining her balance and composure. She flowed with me through the obstacle course as if we'd done this a thousand times. Occasionally, she'd turn her head at a passing song sparrow or to watch me untangle my clothes from a snatching seed head. We arrived at the gate. It was snuggly held shut by a patchwork of rope and wire. I'd been here before when the gate was propped wide open. Today this was the end of the path.

We stood there together at the edge of the property in the warm afternoon sun, watching the landscape. At first, we looked back southwards towards Willow Brook and into the forest of thistles. Our time at the wildlife center together was surely akin to navigating this thorny patch of brambles. Graccia suddenly jerked her attention downward. Automatically trusting her keen senses, my focus followed.

There in the dried grass and leaves was a brown field mouse. He was only a couple steps away, nearly under our noses. Poised on the doorstep of his den, he stood twitching his whiskers at the woman and the hawk. He looked like a country mouse lost in the city of towering thistle stalks. The mouse's brown coat blended in with the groundcover. If it weren't for my sharp-eyed companion I'd easily have missed the daring rodent. The mouse stood, whiskers waving, his black eyes fixed with ours, and then was gone down the hole.

Positive there was more to see on this fine, sunny afternoon, I turned north again and we stood together, taking in the open countryside. I noticed horses grazing two pastures over and others in a corral just upslope. I had never noticed these horses so close by before. I saw a lone woman on horseback traveling down a gravel road I'd never seen before. I took a few deep breaths to draw in the late, auburn sun. I reached up with my bare hand and touched Graccia's feet by lightly laying my fingertips on her smooth yellow toes. As always, she watched my hand, her stare almost cross-eyed down the length of her beak.

Comfortable that we'd seen what we were meant to, I headed back on a lesser-known and less prickly path. Graccia sat still on my weary arm. We passed the bobcat sisters and crossed over the small bridge we'd spent an afternoon on many months ago. I hurried to the A-frame to set her down and give my arm a rest. In the waning light of the day, we stood side by side, quietly, calmly, in good company. I asked her to my glove a few times for bits of quail. We walked to the fencepost and spent some time communing there too.

Now out of ideas grandiose enough for our time together, I decided to escort her back to her mews. Once she was inside, I brought her a live mouse from the tank in the old barn. Graccia, of course, did not pause for a second to pounce on the clueless creature. She grabbed it off the perch in one ferocious leap, scurried to the back of her cage, and turned her back to me. Fluffed up with wings hovered low over the squeaking mouse, Graccia decapitated the mouse swiftly and gorged on the soft organs within the shaking body.

Around sunset a couple days later, everything was cast in a shade of autumn. I shot a few photos of Graccia in her mews. The loud manual shutter of my thirty-year-old camera seemed to startle her as the click bounced off the walls in her small room. Once she was outside on her post the shutter was easily absorbed by the landscape. Graccia paid it no mind. I spent about a half an hour standing at various angles to the gracious hawk, aiming to catch both her mood and the feel of the amber sunlight moving through the trees onto her lovely adult coat. I wanted to remember every inch of her: her sweet little toes, her multi-colored leopard skin cape, her soft cream and russet breast, her daring stare, her divinely red tail. By now she only had one baby brown feather left in that sweeping fan of a tail. This was her at her finest, a radiating, blinding light of joy, love, and gratitude. She was ablaze. She was the goddess of autumn, the angel of fiery red trees and deep golden grasses.

I took off my glove and laid it on the ground for a time. I'm not sure Graccia had ever gotten a chance to see my bare left hand. She was curious to watch how and where it moved. I used this opportunity to snap photos of her turning her head just so as she watched my left hand dance at my side. A flighted red-tail called from above. Graccia cocked her ear towards the voice. I clicked another shot. I turned the lens upward to focus on the dot of a hawk against the clear, blue sky and pressed down on the shutter. The wild hawk drifted up and out of sight. I circled Graccia and captured the last rays of sunlight basking on her tail.

On occasion I asked Graccia to hop to my glove. She chirped and cried over the beloved bits of quail. While she stood on my glove I leaned over and touched my nose to her right wing to draw in her smell. I adored her scent and did this as often as I could think to during our last times together. She smelled like a soft bed, a late summer wind, like leaves crunching under your feet. In those breaths of hawk I'd see mountains from above. The story of the world is told in the aroma of red-tail.

I felt along her smooth toes and ebony talons. I ran my fingers up her keel, dancing them through her thick down. She adoringly nibbled back on my hand. The daylight began to fade and I felt the eyes of the ominous wild great horned owls wandering our way. I went to take her in before her baby cries for food brought the owl's talons to us.

On our next outing together, Graccia and I walked through many of the tasks she had learned during our year together. I asked her to the glove without food and she thought nothing of it. I set her on the scale and she stood there quietly while I read the numbers. I backed her into her travel box and she calmly stepped inside. She did all of these tasks skillfully without food reward. This was the measure of an accomplished ambassador bird. I was pleased. Serving me was apparently reward enough for Graccia. Her weight was surprisingly low and she was very hungry despite the glut of food we'd been serving her. I surmised that she was using a lot of calories trying to generate half a set of primary feathers on one wing. I took her into the clinic kitchen to prepare a mouse to chase the quail she'd already eaten. Her usual apprehension over the clinic was absent. She waited patiently as I thawed and prepped the mouse with my one free hand.

We walked out to the fencepost perch in the dim blue light fading from the day. Usually Graccia was fidgety this time of the evening. I often teased her when she'd get edgy in this light—"we need to get you inside before you turn into a pumpkin." Now it was pumpkin season and Graccia was unconcerned. We stood for a short time, her on the post and me at her side. We faced the three-quarter moon rising over the harvest season. There was a chorus of great horned owl voices carrying from the woods nearby. We listened to the haunting hoots. I kept my eyes sharp for the ghostly owls. I could easily sense that we were walking a razor's edge between the worlds. The remaining refracted sunlight held us in one world and the voices of ghosts beckoned us towards another. I was at once comforted and uneasy. The landscape and moonlight were enchanting. The nearby nighttime predators were disconcerting. I hurriedly called Graccia back and forth from the perch to the glove until her meal was finished, and hastily turned from the dark woods to carry her back to her mews.

I had planned to spend a few more fleeting moments with Graccia the day before her departure. Instead I ended up working the farmstand the whole day to cover for a co-worker who was home sick. It was the first gray, rainy, cold day of fall. I was sad to think that Graccia's last full day on this plane was so dreary. My heart lifted for a moment somewhere around lunchtime as I caught beams of sun pouring into the farm kitchen. I was assured that for at least a few minutes she would get to see the landscape covered in light. Instead of going to visit Graccia after work I wandered home, exhausted.

At home there was a message on my answering machine from Eva. She called to tell me she had a wonderful day with Graccia and she wanted to talk. I'm not even sure I put my keys down before picking up the phone to dial her number. She had spent over four hours bonding with Graccia in the light rain. Eva told me about how they had stood in the corridor lawn visiting with four of the other education birds and their handlers. Papa Rhett was one of their companions, as was Azjnii, a talkative, young great horned owl that Eva had recently took up training. Everyone had a chance to say their goodbyes. At the moment I had noticed the sun shining into the windows at the farm, Graccia had stood on Eva's glove with her wings and tail fanned out, basking in the last light of her days.

≈

I later read the last entry in Graccia's care log penned by Eva:

"11:30a-1:30p and 3p-5:30p. Weight=990 grams. Food= 1 Quail (122 grams). Rainy, cloudy, then sun! Weighed, walk in way outback, stood with other Ed folks, walk in way outback, ground, post, walk. Roused and cried and laughed and cried. A pleasure to be with. So intense on everything she saw and said and did. Enjoyed biding farewell to other ed birds. Graccia has much better more important business to attend to. Had a wonderful time watching. Once rain stopped she spread her feathers out and basked in the sun. She only has one juvenile tail feather left. Beautiful lady. Absolutely fantastic outing, sitting in the rain and basking in the sun. I love her."

∾

As Eva shared her stories of her time with Graccia we both moved into and out of tears. We acknowledged the incredible aching in our chests and the bewildering combination of joy and sorrow. We worked out final plans for the next day. We'd meet in the morning at Willow Brook, say goodbye to Graccia, and then take a trip to the coast to her final resting place. Nowhere in there had I arranged to make up the walk with Graccia I'd missed on this workday. Eva pleaded with me to go see Graccia, if only for a half an hour. I admitted that I would feel bad taking her out without being able to offer her any food, because after all, that was one of her greatest joys. She couldn't eat within twenty-four hours of the euthanasia to prevent complications. Eva argued that Graccia was perfectly happy going for hours without food during their outing.

Eva insisted that Graccia's last walk needed to be with me. I agreed with her and let go of my feeble attempt to avoid a painfully raw experience. When you know a loved one's moments on this earth are numbered, you've already lost the ability to see them incarnate. As you breathe the same air they do, you, like them, are no longer in your body. Part of you starts to leave with them. If it weren't for that paralyzing heartache constantly pulling your consciousness back, part of you probably would go with them.

~

PART THREE

The Pink Blanket

~

❧ 13 ❧

The Yellow Butterfly

I woke up on the morning of the summer solstice imme-diately thinking that Thalia had a few short hours left in this world. I solemnly went about my morning, eating breakfast and tidying up the house. At about 10:30 a.m. I started gathering all I needed for the day. A few pieces of leftover homemade pizza, some toasted hazelnuts, and a bottle of water made up my sack lunch. In the spare bed-room, I took my black hip-pack out of the closet. Thalia's body would go in there for the walk into the marsh.

"That bag went with me all over the island," I said out loud to myself, "how strange it is that I randomly decided on it a couple days ago." *Should I wear a hair scarf or a hat?* I wondered. I went to the coat closet and picked out a baseball hat. Then I went to the bathroom and glanced in the mirror. I saw the jaguar stitched on the front and chuckled. We'd need the big cats with us today.

I felt like I was walking through a dream, performing some sort of preordained ritual I hadn't begun to imagine. After collecting my sage smudge, lighter, and rattle, I was driving out to Willow Brook. I was numb, nearly out of my body with fear. At the clinic, I stood outside the usual mayhem. People were going this way and that. Someone was spraying laundry outside. Another volunteer was shouting questions from the ICU. Answers were coming from my co-worker in the kitchen. She was busy worrying over food charts. Ian walked in the front door and passed through the chaos. I can still see the look on his face. It was as if everything else kept moving around his unwavering, somber mood.

He approached me and quietly asked, "How do you want to do this?"

I hadn't had Thalia on my glove outside her mews for weeks and I didn't think I would be able to convince her to join me for a walk. To get her on my glove and out of her mews I would likely have to resort to trickery. I couldn't fathom deceiving my dear friend, not at a time like this. The other option was that I could go in her cage with a towel and gloves on both hands. I would have to use all of my predatory nature to snare the flighty harrier and hold her screaming in my arms as I wrapped her in a towel. I just couldn't bring myself to attack her in this way. We'd struggled against each other enough already. Now was a time for release.

"Why don't you go ahead and go get her?" I responded to Ian. He looked at me in a split second of compassion and inner turmoil. I could tell he too didn't feel like catching the hawk because he knew how much she hated it. With that he went to a cupboard, opened the door, and took out a set of brand new elbow-length Kevlar gloves. When catching raptors, even eagles, Ian usually wore a worn out pair of blue welding gloves that barely reached past his wrists.

"Why you're using those brand new black gloves is beyond me," I prodded.

"Well, they're not so new anymore," he joked to my co-worker Zoe and me. "Look at this streak of guano on this glove."

Enjoying the moment of mindless banter, I replied, "How could a pair of gloves used to catch wild animals possibly stay clean?"

With that he turned to walk out to Thalia's cage. The agony was so strong in my chest that I hadn't been able to bring myself to visit her that morning. I was terrified. Sensing my anguish, my co-worker, Zoe, offered to go over our work schedule and discuss some of the cases. I met her eyes and took the invitation to ignore the tightness in my chest. We talked until she was called to help with a new patient and I set to sorting out paperwork. Ian was gone for longer than expected. Part of me was glad for the chance to pretend I was living a different day. The rest of me wanted to break through this wall into my life beyond. Zoe and I were mid-sentence when Ian walked through the door.

Reality came in flashes. I saw Thalia's sweet ankles held tight between Ian's left fingers. Her talons were curled. There was my favorite shade of gold and those flashy black talons. Ian's face was fraught with struggle. "She gave me quite a run for my money," he complained, clearly wishing there was a different way. I searched desperately to connect to the experience. I scrambled tirelessly to avoid it. Thalia was wrapped in a pink blanket, cradled in Ian's left arm. I couldn't see any of her feathers, just those harrier legs. They seemed completely out of context.

Ian rushed into the treatment room and reached with his right hand over to uncover Thalia's head only slightly. I still couldn't see her face. My disbelief held strong. He stretched his arm across his body to grab the piping that led to the isoflorene machine. He put the cup over her beak and turned the knobs of the machine on. I moved around Ian so I could peer into Thalia's amber eyes. At first they were locked open in fear, but then they began to blink from exhaustion.

Ian stood there, firmly and gently holding Thalia in his arms. "I feel guilty," he confessed.

"For what?" I asked, "bringing her into this life?"

"No," he replied, "for all the anguish she's suffered. Maybe if she'd had one handler and one home all this time she'd be okay."

I knew I couldn't meet his hypothetical situation head on with rationale and case studies. The mind couldn't explain what the heart had to admit. I phrased my response as best I could. "It was amazing how much she changed when I gave her the live mice. The hunter was just right there on the surface."

Ian smiled at me in understanding.

Thalia drifted further into sleep, her eyes were closed more than open now.

"What was the story with the harrier nestling that came in three days ago?" I asked Ian. Before he had brought Thalia in I had found the paperwork for the northern harrier nestling. We rarely had harriers come into the center, so I knew this was an omen.

"A haying machine had gone over its nest and tore its right wing entirely off," he replied. That was the same wing of Thalia's that was handicapped. "A couple years ago I may have considered keeping the nestling as an education bird, but after this experience with Thalia there is no way. All we could do was put it down."

I sighed a breath of relief. Some creatures were best left to the wild. Thalia was sound asleep now. Ian let go of her long, limp legs and passed her body onto the table. With one hand on the cup on her beak, he used his free hand to open the pink blanket. My denial was shattered.

Her chest heaved in full, deep breaths. Ian ran the tips of his fingers along her cream and russet streaked breast feathers. I took my turn to do the same, the nerves in my fingers sending messages into the depths of my soul.

Ian carefully positioned Thalia's head so that the isoflorene cup rested alone on her beak. He took out a pair of scissors and laid them on the table. Next he deliberately pulled the leather jesses out of the grommets in each of her anklets and laid them at her feet. "She won't need these anymore," he mumbled to himself as he used the scissors to snip the anklets off her legs. He was handing her life over to her.

Tears rolled off my cheeks. I couldn't look up to see Ian's face. I was too busy trying to grieve gracefully, trying to hold my spirit from following hers. Where would my life be without her in it? He stroked her belly of feathers lightly a few more times, then wrapped her in the pink blanket. I left the room. Either I wasn't sure I could hold myself together or I felt she was already on her way. Earlier in the morning while I was preparing for the day I'd had a clear vision of her bursting out of her body and flying up into the sky. The image came back to me and I knew my friend was on her way. I had to keep my feet in this world.

I decided I had some time while Thalia's body fully came to rest. I pulled out the toolbox and got out what I need to repair the cage wall I'd torn open to release the trapped spotted towhee the night before. If I could help it, no one was going to get themselves into that mess again. Ian walked with me to the cage.

"What do you plan to do with Thalia's body?" he asked.

"I'm going to take her to the wildlife refuge south of town and walk a long ways down a trail. Then I'm

going to leave her body deep in the reeds of the marsh."
I answered.

He responded with silence. I tried not to doubt my
plans. Luckily, the sunshine and lush, green enfoldment
of the surrounding foliage were able to hold the pieces of
my heart together. Ian and I parted ways, and I propped
a stepladder up next to the cage. The screen was a quick
and easy fix, but when I finished I realized that the day
was getting on. The sun was high in the sky and the heat
of summer pushed against my skin. I wandered back up
to gather Thalia and carry on my way. Inside the clinic,
Ian tapped on a shoebox and said, "here's Thalia" before
carrying on with managing patient care. I put the feather-
light box under my arm and went up to my car.

As I went to pull out of the driveway, I turned on my
blinker and looked left. An entire construction crew had
set up in the time I'd been at Willow Brook. Deciding not
to fuss with a flagger and long wait, I turned right to go a
different route.

On this day, nothing happened by mistake. Within
a half mile of the wildlife center, I was passing a ripe
golden field. There was a haying machine busily mowing the golden pasture. I thought back to my life purpose journey and the endless fields of wheat stubble that
stood between myself and my purpose. This was the same
kind of machine that had cut Thalia off from a life in the
wild and that had severed the wing of the harrier nestling
brought into Willow Brook days before. The mechaniza-
tion of the modern world had separated us all from living the true, wild purpose nature intended for our souls.
This knowing came into my being at the time without
the words to explain.

I kept an eye out for more messages on my drive
south, but downtown looked as bland and gray as usual.

Once I was back out in the open countryside, a red-tailed hawk passed over the highway just in front of my car. She was flapping hard towards a field of cut clover. A month or two ago that field had been a stunning ocean of red blossoms. The cut fields added to the experience by lending me the sense that everything had come full circle for Thalia. This was the time of year when she would have hatched from her egg, grown strong in the nest, and lifted off to the freedom her soul had right to. Something that was wrong in the world was being set in balance.

At last, I came to the road into the marsh and turned onto the gravel. Apprehension visited me again. I could feel the tension writhing in my veins. Would I be able to find a proper resting place for Thalia's body? My plan to take her into the marsh was not founded on any knowledge about the terrain in the wetlands. I had no idea if I could find a spot out of view of farmhouses, roads, and hikers. Her body had to be left inaccessible. I needed to be alone with her in the reeds.

I choose the third parking lot along the road that was just across a bridge over the marsh. I had crossed over into another world. The parking lot was empty. The dust on the road settled. Already I was seeing great blue herons everywhere. I lingered in the car, tears streaming down my face. I didn't think I could bring myself to do this. I was terrified of letting the reality of Thalia's passing sink in. There was no way I could walk away from her until I had a tangible experience with her passing and a chance to honor her infinite spirit.

I took a deep breath and looked up from the palms of my hands and wads of tissue. Something shifted. I felt a wave of comfort and protection flow through my body. This was my cue to check inward and look beyond the mundane. In my mind's eye I saw a black panther's broad face with glowing green eyes poke up just above the passenger door. I swore I heard him say, "let's get going."

Reluctantly, I started loading my things into the black bag. "Come on. Get going," he urged. I put my water bottle in a pocket. "Let's go!" he pleaded. I wiped my tears, blew my nose and looked outside my window.

There stood cougar. "It's time to go now."

"Okay, I'm coming," I answered out loud, reaching over to the silent shoebox to lift the lid. With both hands I clutched the body in the pink blanket, slipped the bundle into my bag, and pulled the zipper shut. I heaved myself out of the car seat, locked the door, slung the bag over my shoulder, and secured the belt of the bag around my waist. We were off.

I could feel and see in my mind panther and cougar following behind me like tailgaters making sure I didn't lag behind. I wandered off the main road to a gauge station to stand gazing over the open water of the wetland. Part of me still wanted to pretend I was out there for some leisurely bird watching. Cougar and panther waited impatiently for me on the dirt path.

As I walked in the hot mid-day sun, herons lifted out of the cattails every few minutes, disturbed by my intrusion into their realm. On occasion one would let out a loud, gruff grunt. I reminded myself that I had learned in *Medicine Cards* by Jamie Sams and David Carson that blue herons symbolize self-reflection. There were dense woods to my left and open marsh to my right. I kept tripping on some soil stabilization netting that a well-meaning wildlife area manager had buried. It was now exposed by rain and wind. I couldn't help but worry about the hazard it posed to wildlife of all sorts. After months of caring for wildlife sick, injured, and orphaned due to the side effects of urbanization, any human invention looked like a hazard to me.

I knew I wanted to be out of sight of the road I'd driven in on, so I kept walking toward a leafless line of trees. I hoped for an open but secluded expanse of marsh on the other side of the trees. I dreaded more trees beyond those. I continued at a steady pace. Just then, a horrendous crashing within a few feet of me sent me reeling backwards. It was merely another enormous blue heron. He flapped off, drawing his legs up and his neck into his body. I paused to listen to a croaking frog. The brown and wilted vegetation in this spot encouraged me to continue on for lusher habitat.

I walked past the line of trees to find a whole new, concealed marsh laid out in front of me. I looked back the way I'd come. The road was no longer in sight. This marshland was lush green with a circle of tall trees skirting the edges. I was definitely in prime harrier habitat and could rest easy. I was nearing the end of my journey.

The problem was that I'd come to a fork in the road. One path continued north away from the public road and the other ran east along the line of sparsely leaved trees. My logic said to go north away from the people, but instead I decided to ask panther and cougar for guidance. I looked through this world and inward in the same moment to see the big cats stream eastward. My feet followed them to the right.

At this point, all that remained was for me to find a place to leave Thalia's body. I walked a mere two hundred yards or so before sensing I'd reached my destination. I looked up past the reeds and into the open water. There an old snag lay in the water. "That looks like a great place for a harrier to perch," I thought to myself while watching a red-winged blackbird do a mating display on the log. The red and yellow patches on his wings flashed bright like fire amidst his gleaming black coat. I smiled in gratitude for his reassurance.

The buckle of my bag came unsnapped in my fingers. I lifted the shoulder strap over my head, laid the bag on the ground, and paused to take a drink of water. The heat finally graced the dark sadness in my heart. I was getting warm. I reached into my bag and lifted the sacred bundle that held my friend out to lay her on the grass beside the trail. "Here we are, big girl."

My words were answered with a strange rasping birdcall overhead. I jerked my face upwards and saw the brown figure of a bittern fly by. Bitterns are nearly as big as great blue herons, but twice as secretive as herons are boisterous. What a rare treat to see such a myth of the marsh in broad daylight and raging heat. It was time to begin the ceremony.

Thalia's body was still wrapped snug in the soft pink blanket. I lit a bundle of sage and cedar and knelt down to fan the fragrant smoke over her with my hands. Over and over I fanned. Again and again I asked the spirits to cleanse the pain of the body from the spirit of this hawk. My insistence underpinned how important I knew this ritual was for Thalia. She deserved to be free of this crippled body. She had been in service long enough.

I stood up to face each of the directions and offered the smoke of the sacred herbs. I smudged myself as well in the hopes that I too could be cleansed of the pain of the years spent living estranged from my true self. I then offered smoke upwards to Father Sky and down onto Mother Earth. It seemed the wind picked up when I began my intimate ceremony. Now the herb bunch burned freely. I took a few steps down the trail to clear some vegetation away from the ground and rubbed the tip of the burning smudge into the dirt.

Next, I shook my egg-shaped hand rattle while facing each of the cardinal directions, inviting the spirits to assist Thalia in her flight to the afterlife and the freedom beyond. To bring the gifts of each of the directions to Thalia, I finished by rattling over her body. No one had ever taught me how to do ceremony before, let alone a funeral. This was all I could think to do in the moment, just these few simple things. It didn't matter that I was relatively short-versed or that I had no idea why I felt compelled to honor Thalia in this way. I was able act openly from the heart. This was how Thalia would appreciate it.

My few ceremonial tools went back into my bag one at a time in gratitude for the service and support they'd offered. I turned back to the pink package resting quietly on the ground and knelt exhausted at her feet. One corner at a time, I lifted the blanket from the casing of feathers, flesh, and bones that had served Thalia in her four years of this life. I picked her up into the palms of both my hands and walked into the six-foot high reeds and grass.

At the water's edge I looked down into the woven web of grass. For a few moments I stood with her stroking the burnt amber and cream feathers on her breast. With my right hand I cradled her lifeless head and lifted her face up to mine. The downy white lids covering her eyes were new to me. They were not closed all of the way and I could see the light in her eyes through a tiny crack. I gently tried to close her eyes completely, but the fissure of light demanded to come through.

Words flowed from my lips to accompany the tears that dripped off my cheeks onto her soft coat. "There will be no more pain for you. You are now free. I'm sorry for the fear and pain you suffered, but now you are free. It's time to go back now, it's time to go back."

I was not grieving for the loss of the maiden harrier. I was weeping for the loss of spirit she suffered in this life. Over the course of our relationship, many times when I cried I felt her pain release with my own. I was the hollow reed through which her pain could move out. The movement of her anguish in turn cleansed my own suffering. The pain was immense and the release was necessary. I'd had a broken heart countless times before in my life, but this aching was something different. I was not worried about missing her or the love between us being severed. I just felt the pain, sorrow, and suffering move into and out of me through the tears. I cried from relief and joy, for I could truly release her now. I too was free from the burden of holding her captive.

Once I said all I needed to, aloud and unspoken, I bent over to part the woven marsh grass. I was passing her body through the veil and back into the earth. She lay cradled in the mud of the mother, offered back to the source of all life with unending gratitude. I then did my best to re-weave the grass and thus mend the hole in the tapestry left open when this wild spirit was taken from her place in the natural order of things.

"Goodbye my love, goodbye beloved one."

I turned and walked away. On the dirt path, I picked up the blanket and had a sense that some of her spirit was still wrapped into the fabric. My intuition told me to lay the blanket back on the earth and sit on it cross-legged for a few moments. Not knowing why I sat there, I turned into a hollow reed. I was the path that allowed that last bit of spirit to leave. I felt it course out through the top of my head. I stood up, picked up the small blanket, and held it in both hands. With a sharp snap my hands shook the bits of remaining energy free. A group of ducks in the channel beneath the leafless trees burst into the air in a deafening whir of wings. It felt like Thalia lifting off. My muscles settled in the release.

With everything accomplished as far as I could tell, I shouldered my lighter load to head back to my car. Black-headed grosbeaks sang a rambling melody as I walked and an American goldfinch fluttered across my path. The world seemed cheerier and lighter. I slipped into the driver's seat and picked out a new CD to listen to and turned the key in the ignition.

A yellow butterfly fluttered across my windshield, inches from my face.

I flashed back to a couple of weeks ago. I stood in the clinic kitchen of Willow Brook holding a mangled feather in my fingers. It was one of Thalia's feathers that had broken off her right wing. I had found it lying in the gravel of her mews. Sections of the feather were still locked in the shaft, hardened and unfurled. I knew this feather meant something and was puzzling over it when a dear friend of mine who volunteered at the center offered an insightful interpretation.

"Have you ever heard of a butterfly's wings hardening?" she asked.

"No, I haven't," I replied.

"When I was a little girl my sister and I used to bring caterpillars into the house to watch them spin cocoons and hatch out as butterflies. My mother, a biologist, always warned us to give the hatching butterflies plenty of space. She told us that if the butterflies didn't have enough space to spread open their wings when fresh out of the cocoon that their wings would dry hard in a cramped position and they wouldn't be able to fly free."

I understood the piece of wisdom my friend had to offer. Thalia didn't have enough space to spread her wings and fly. No cage could have been large enough. I knew that now.

With a smile radiating out from my heart I shifted the car into reverse, turned the wheel, and backed the car out in a big arch. The gravel crunched busily under the tires. "You could have it all if you could gracefully let go . . ." sang the singer on my CD. I pushed in the clutch and shifted into first gear, ready to pull out onto the gravel road.

Looking out to the marsh across the road, a mob of blackbirds filled my entire field of view. They were attacking a hawk. In powerful, courageous strokes, the raptor was launching straight up from the water's surface. I couldn't believe my eyes. Was this a northern harrier?

Instinctively, I focused on the rump of the bird. Glaring right back at me was a solid white patch at the base of the brown bird's tail. *Brown bird*, I thought to myself. This time of year this harrier was most likely a female. She was flying straight away from me, so I didn't get a chance to see her chest and confirm my hunch. A ways in front of the harrier there was another, but it was too far off for me to identify. Could it have been her mate? I could only imagine.

The scene was exactly where my imagination would have placed Thalia. She'd be out terrorizing the marsh, digging up trouble and tearing around. She'd have a family to tend to. The two hawks flew up and over a dense wood and were gone too quickly. I was left sitting there with the sound of the angry mob of blackbirds still ringing in my ears. Somewhere along the way I had managed to turn off the music. The marsh wrens settled back into talking calmly in harsh, raspy tones. A hot summer breeze hit my face through the window. I took a deep breath, whispered "goodbye Thalia," turned up the stereo, and turned down the gravel road.

Later in the day, I went on a trip to the coast with my husband, Chris, and my yellow lab, Buckwheat, to have a solstice bonfire. We collected kindling from alongside the highway and found driftwood on the beach. Buckwheat had a short swim in the cold, gray surf before we began to work on the fire. There was a thick marine layer hanging on to the coastline, but the fire started quickly and kept us warm almost instantly. We set our dinner on the coals and watched the last few beach strollers straggle off into the houses behind the dunes. Soon enough, we were alone and the last light of the longest day was gone. My final ritual of the day was to pull out Thalia's mangled feather from my black bag. I twirled it in my fingertips and remembered the yellow butterfly. I reached over the hot flames and dropped the feather into the center of the fire.

≈ 14 ≈

When the Hawk Covers the Earth

I woke up greeted by an early morning mist. It lay thick on the valley and held morning bird song at bay. I smiled, thinking of my wedding day and the magic of mist. Spirits find safe passage in the between land of fog. Then the ache in my heart flowed to the tips of my toes and the crown of my head. The gravity of the day weighed bitter. I pulled myself together, covered my sore body with a wool shawl, and walked out the front door alone. Despite full daylight, it seemed the whole world was asleep. Was I still dreaming?

I softly opened the gate to the Willow Brook center and drifted down the worn road. I couldn't feel the gravel under my soles or the autumn frost in the air. The sun began to peak over the horizon. The mist still hung low, now backlit. I could barely lift my heavy feet up the few stairs into the clinic. Inside, I turned on the lights, but no one was home. I found a place to leave my belongings. I wished I could leave all material behind and walk off into another life.

I floated into the kitchen without pulling food out of the freezer, part of our routine already gone. In the raptor barn cupboards I found my black glove still on loan from Annie, the woman who'd trained me to work with Thalia. I pulled out my particular swivel, hidden in the same spot as always. I borrowed the great horned owl Tskili's leash as usual. Each act I compelled my muscles to perform was hopelessly arduous. The simple latch on the mews door proved challenging. I looked down to see the pouch for hiding my fears dangling from the doorknob and didn't have the heart to put it in my pocket just yet.

Graccia stood with her back to me as I gradually stepped inside her room. I know she felt my anguish. I choose to let her know how much she'd be missed. She faced westward through the bars of her window. I mustered as light a voice as I could and tried not to let my voice crack, "Hello Miss Graccia, good morning."

She turned to greet me. I cautiously approached, wearing my worry on my sleeve. We both knew what was coming and I was the main agent bringing the end. Would we be able to enjoy each other's company in the brief seconds until then? When I raised my glove to ask her on, she timidly moved away. I took a few steps towards her and she moved again. Now she held her wings out and looked like she was going to try and jump away from me. I lowered my arm and took a deep breath. I had no choice but to let go of the excruciating guilt I was carrying. With a simple thought it was gone.

Graccia turned to me, folded her wings back in, and waited. I raised my glove, and without a word from my lips she stepped up. I effortlessly moved the swivel through the holes in her rain dried jesses. I attached the leash and wrapped it twice around my two bottom fingers, and once around my bottom three fingers. It felt just like tying my shoes in the morning. We exited her mews. Graccia became restless in the hallway. I literally felt her energy pulling back into her mews. I realized that I hadn't given her a chance to say goodbye. We turned to stand outside the door, both looking in. I voiced our sentiments to the space. "Thank you for providing such a good home for Graccia."

She relaxed and we moved through the dark hallway and out into the increasing light of day. I carried her down the road to the post and, unable to bear my heartache, I placed her on the post so I could take another deep breath. The guilt was hard to shake and the grief was consuming. Graccia stood, content but chilled. Her body shivered in the crisp morning air. She puffed out her coat to hold in the warmth emanating from her core.

I clutched my shawl closed and stood, memorizing every single feather on her body. Each was as unique as a snowflake. Then, like peering through a looking glass, I noticed a figure on one of the contour feathers among those in her belly. It was in the shape of a spirit, much like that of an angel. The spirit's arms were straight out and it wore a long flowing robe that extended across the tip of Graccia's feather. I took a step back and widened my focus. Before me stood a gathering of angels spanning the width of her breast. As I absorbed the entire picture I was without breath. Below the feathers painted with spirits were feathers hatched with horizontal lines. In reading the story written there, I saw that these markings represented the earth. The earth lines rose to form a fleet of spirits that looked like robed angels with arms outstretched. The spirit fleet then morphed into vertical lines, beings of light, shooting into the heavens. The pattern was so plainly written at this moment outside time. The story told on her breast was that of enlightened beings that are born of the earth and then merged with the heavens.

As the mist melted in the sunshine, further knowing flowed into my soul. The gate was opening. Graccia had more spirits painted on the side of her breast closest to her injured wing. During her short time on this plane she had helped both Eva and I heal by showing us how to connect with the earth and the stars. She had given her flight, her life, to this purpose. Why had she chosen us? All I knew is that we were willing to listen.

I now understood why I felt compelled to bury her on the farm my friends owned on the coast. They planned to develop a spiritual healing center there for retreats and workshops. The land would serve as a place of healing, meditation, and reprieve. People would visit to connect with the spirit of the land and to gaze up into a sky full of stars. Graccia would be in fond company.

The gracious hawk interrupted my euphoria with an honest yawn. It broke the gravity of the moment. I began taking regular breaths again. She opened up her mouth and turned her head downwards. As she shook her head, out came a pellet. It fell to the ground. It was only about the circumference of a quarter. She looked up at me and then back down at the pellet as if to say, "This is my gift to you."

I chuckled and smiled, "Well thank you, but that's kinda gross!"

I bent over and pulled the sticky wad of quail bones and feathers from the dew-soaked grass. I carefully placed it on a large fallen leaf and made a mental note of where I'd left it. Then she looked at me with her "Okay, I'm ready to eat" face. I must have communicated well enough with my look back that I didn't have food because she immediately relaxed back into watching the day go by. By now the fog had mostly cleared and the sun was above the horizon.

I looked up the road and saw Eva come through the gate. As she approached I could see the grief in her face. Like a mirror, I reflected back my own sorrow. We broke down sobbing into each other's arms. Graccia stood towering over us. Unwilling to dive into the depths of this well, I pulled back, took a deep breath again, and wiped the tears off my face. My time to bask in Graccia's company was short. I reached into my will and pushed up courage. It was time to speak. Graccia was still a fluffball—warm as could be. I was able to point out the story written on her breast.

"Look at this," I said to Eva, directing her attention as I went. "See the horizontal lines that represent the earth? And the figures of the spirits in robes? And the streaks of light going to the heavens? Can you believe we've never noticed this before?"

Eva stood, shaking her head. "That's amazing." I was relieved because I had been afraid I was the only one who would be able to see it. It's hard to point out an elephant made of the shifting clouds. I leaned down to pick up the gooey pellet from atop the leaf and held it out for Eva to see. "Look at the gift Graccia just gave me," I said with a smirk on my face. We erupted in laughter between tears.

"That can go in the rattle I'm making for you," Eva replied. I handed it to her for safekeeping. I picked up my glove off the ground and slid my hand inside. We stood there together for one last moment, and then I reached up and asked Graccia onto my glove. We quietly turned and made our way to the clinic.

Eva was the first in and left the door open for us to enter. I brought Graccia through the kitchen, down the hallway, and into the ICU to the first home she'd ever known at Willow Brook. I opened the door to the small wooden box. Memories flashed of our first encounters with the sweet juvenile red-tail full of wonder. She stepped onto the perch and stood staring out, calm as her first day here. I swiveled the door closed, fastened the latch, and walked into the hallway where Eva was standing. She pointed to a large photo of Graccia she'd taken during their hours in the rain. Eva posted it in the "Above and Beyond Commitment Award" section of the clinic whiteboard. Underneath she wrote, "There is no death, only walking into other worlds." By now it was just as painful to hold back the tears as it was to swim in them.

"I have two blankets for you to choose from," Eva said as she grabbed a shopping bag. I remembered that I had asked her if she could pick up a pink blanket to bury Graccia in. I held the two baby blankets in my hands and quickly choose the softest blanket I had ever felt. On one end there was a bunny hugging a heart stitched on a patch of silk. It was perfect.

Our friend Ginger came through the front door of the clinic with tears in her eyes and hawk earrings hanging from her earlobes. I remembered that I had asked her if she could join us. Even though she rarely spent time with Graccia, she knew the hawk well because we had been close friends throughout my year with Graccia. Ginger also attended the gatherings at my house. Eva and I reached up and pointed to the photo. The tears welled in Ginger's eyes as she told us about a hawk she'd worked with years ago. Her hawk had also lived a short life. We stood in a tight circle in the small hallway, holding each other up, struggling not to succumb to absolute despair. The despondency in my chest was suffocating. I surfaced, drawing in my hundredth deep breath, and led the way down the hall.

We stood and watched Graccia in her small wooden box watching us. Here was the answer to my dreams, my best friend. This was the worst moment of my life. It was all I could do to not fracture into a thousand pieces. My love for her held me present. My place was here by her side. I put my glove back on my hand and opened the door. She sat still, waiting for my request. I asked her onto the glove and she confidently moved on. I felt her weight sink into my hand. I lifted her out of the box and attached the swivel and leash. We stood with her in complete admiration. What a gorgeous spirit, a brilliant light.

I motioned to Ginger to step outside the room and Eva spread the soft, pink blanket between her hands. Graccia, knowing we were about to grab her, kicked in to survival mode and began to fuss, but Eva was able to get a hold of Graccia before she jumped off the glove. I swiftly moved to help Eva secure Graccia in the blanket and, once everyone was calm, I took the swivel and leash back off of her jesses. The routine of tending to usual tasks held a glimmer of normalcy in such a bizarre situation. Eva carried her into the treatment room. She laid her on the table she'd covered with a pink towel. I moved to the gas machine and turned it on, checking with Eva to make sure I had the settings correct. My vision was blurry. About this time, Ian came in the front door. Ginger moved out of the treatment room to greet him, shutting the door behind her.

The three of us sisters were alone. I looked up to meet Eva's eyes and nodded. She dropped her chin in agreement. In my left hand, I picked up the cup at the end of the tube full of isoflorane gas. With Eva's help I uncovered Graccia's head with my right hand. I put the cup over her beak and she bit at the plastic. Within a few breaths her bright eyes became weary. The light began to fade. She was drifting off to sleep. Her eyelids grew heavy and her eyes closed, never to see to the light of day again. Eva and I uncovered her body and I read the following prayer aloud while untying the jesses from her ankles:

> With overwhelming, unending gratitude we release you. We release you from this body high into the heavens. High in the heavens shall your spirit soar.
>
> May your infinite joy lift you up with the spirits. May the spirits surround you and heal you. May they guide you on your purposeful journey.
>
> We give love and gratitude that we are part of that journey. To know you is to know the joy of all hearts at once. All joy in one feathered soul. Gracious One.
>
> Gracious One, we release you.
>
> We release you, we love you, we are you, thank you, Gracious One.

The room fell silent. I felt with a heavy heart and saw with blurry eyes Graccia's spirit lift from her body and hover above us. Her body was so still now. Eva ran her fingertips through the soft down in Graccia's belly. I cupped my hands around the gracious hawk's cold feet. I took a few gasping breaths for air, fighting against the excruciating pain in my chest, and reached across her body to pull the blanket around her. I checked in with Eva to make sure she was ready. Through the tears in her eyes she found the strength to nod. I wrapped Graccia in the soft, pink blanket. I pulled her limp body off the table and into my arms. I clutched her tightly to my breast. The pain cleared my chest for the first time in days. It was if that by an unimaginable act of kindness that Graccia agreed to carry my anguish with her to the other side. That was it. It was done.

I went outside where Ginger was waiting for me. Owl hoots wandered to us from the woods. This was a likely day for these creatures of the night to be chatting. The great horned owls erupted into a chorus of hoots. The air was filled with their haunting song. Eva joined us, turned her ears to the woods, and said, "owls call the spirits to the other side." A turkey vulture flew low and to the north, wobbling in the wind. I looked into his eyes and saw that he was here for the same occasion.

I went back inside, placed Graccia's body in a carrier for transport home, and grabbed my drum bag and the white mouse I'd packaged for Graccia to carry with her to the other side. Eva, Ginger, and I wandered to the parking lot and exchanged hugs. I placed the carrier in my back seat and drove the few miles home in tears. The day had only just begun.

Eva and I met back at my house. We were there to pick up Chris, Buckwheat, and a few ceremonial supplies before heading out to the coast. We loaded our goods into Eva's car, including a cooler full of food. I lifted Graccia's body from the carrier and wrapped it and her mouse in my wool sun deity blanket. I lovingly carried her body to the vehicle and gently laid her behind the driver's seat. Buckwheat stood out on the driveway, tail wagging. He knew a day with friends was in store and for him life was good. I tapped on the back bumper of the hatchback and supported his back legs as he pulled himself in by his arms. The days of limber joints were gone for our old boy. He tucked himself in against the backseat. I waited for his tail to clear the door and pulled it shut. Chris got in the back and I hopped into my place up front beside Eva. We drove through town, making small talk and searching through Eva's CD collection. What music was fitting for such a day? My guess was some *Best of John Denver*. Apparently I made a good choice, because the car was full of stories and laughter by the time we made it to the fork in the road.

"Which way should we go?" Eva asked.

"Definitely the scenic route," Chris and I answered. On a somber but sunny day like this a slow, meandering road was just the cure. We noticed the very birth of fall colors painting the hillsides. The fields were dry and golden. The air was crisp and sky was brilliant blue.

"Thank God it is so gorgeous today," I remarked, "I have no idea how I'd make it if it was pouring rain."

"I hear you," Eva answered with a sigh.

We sat silent and introspective until a song made Chris think of something curious and he started conversation back up. We moved into and out of sadness and smiles in this way and greeted the wild red-tailed hawks we saw along the drive. Some were soaring while others sat on telephone poles watching our car go by. Each sighting was bittersweet. We came along a river and Buckwheat lifted his nose in the air to smell the water. When we got to the beach, he was on his feet in the back of the car.

"We can't stop today," I said to him with a twinge of remorse. I loved to watch him run in the sand and low tides. We turned away from the coastline and followed the river into the woods. I spotted a red-tail soaring over the valley just below our destination, and Eva pulled the car over. Each of us peered out the windows and marveled at the gift of flight on broad wings. We then continued to direct Eva along back roads to our friends' farm. They were away for the weekend, but had extended an open invitation for us to come. I was eternally grateful that they'd given me permission to bury Graccia here, but was also sad that they'd never gotten a chance to meet her. We stopped to talk with the housesitter at the gate of the property before going up to the house. He was leaving for the day, so we had the place to ourselves.

When we walked in the front door I noticed how chilly the house was without the aroma of fantastic food and the warmth of the oven. Chris and I both remarked that it was sad to see the place empty. We dropped off the cooler in the kitchen and quickly moved back outside. Buckwheat was already out wandering, formulating a place history with his nose. We called him to the car, where I was busy pulling out what I needed.

"What can we carry?" Chris asked. I stuck my hand out of the car with a bag of journals in hand. He shouldered it, along with the shovel he'd found in a shed nearby, and asked for more.

"I'm good," I responded, hefting my drum bag over my shoulder and lifting the blanket that held Graccia's body into my arms. Eva shut the car door and we began our hike down the road to Graccia's final resting place. Buckwheat trotted ahead, tail high. We made our way past the orchard, tool sheds, and old homestead. Chris and I pointed out the heirloom berry garden to Eva. It was too late in the year to stop for a handful of berries. Next, we passed the poultry houses and yards. We couldn't help but pause and marvel at the obnoxiously loud gander yelling his head off at us. I chuckled and commented, "Graccia had those noisy ducks, chickens, and turkeys just out her window at Willow Brook. Now her body will rest near familiar sounds."

The canopy of the ancient grove of Douglas firs was a short ways away. When we stepped under the shadows of the giants the mood of the day changed completely. Now words were only used when absolutely necessary. Both Chris and Eva turned to look at me. I could see by the expressions on their faces that they wanted to know where to go. I walked up to the grandfather tree that carried me to other worlds. I stood there in his presence, feeling lost.

"How about we look for someplace around here that is free of ferns and red huckleberry bushes so we don't have to uproot any plants?" Chris offered.

"That's a great idea," I said, watching him walk directly to the perfect spot. "That will work, Chris." Eva nodded in agreement and Chris knelt down to remove the mat of moss that covered the earth in the spot. I set down my bag and the bundle of Graccia's body. Chris set the moss aside so that we could lay it back over the grave when we were finished. I got out my sage smudge and set to clearing each of us, including Buckwheat. Chris picked up the shovel and began digging. Eva stood in adoration of the old growth trees while we waited for Chris to finish working. When he was done, he set the shovel against a tree and joined us just upslope of the grave. I pulled out my journals and searched for a few entries to read.

My first passage was from my initial meeting with Graccia, the curious youngster staring out of her cage at me. I turned open the book to the right page and looked at the date. I saw that the entry was exactly one year ago to the day. I hadn't made this connection before. Stunned, I looked up to point out this synchronous timing to Eva and Chris. Next, I read about retrieving a power animal for Graccia our busy little beaver. And last I pulled out Sandra Ingerman's *Medicine for the Earth* and read the following:

> Regeneration is a part of life. As we don't always know what little deaths are part of our destiny, we must put our trust and faith in our spirit and the power of the universe to help us release that which no longer serves us. Our only role during this time is to be like the tree who remembers its true nature and gracefully lets go of its leaves to return to the earth.

I turned back to face Buckwheat, who sat just outside our circle. He sat still as a statue staring solemnly forward. When we moved he remained. At nearly eleven years old, he rarely sat for long. His joints would get stiff and he'd either lie down or get up and sniff around. During the entire memorial ceremony he sat with an overpowering air of reverence on his face. I was humbled by his solemn expression of compassion and love. I sent him a message of gratitude and knelt at Graccia's body, still wrapped in layers of blankets.

I unfolded my wool blanket, exposing the soft, pink blanket underneath. Eva walked up and picked up Graccia in her arms, cradling her in the plush blanket. This was the first she'd held her since placing her on the treatment table at Willow Brook. Eva clutched the gracious hawk's body to her chest and took long deep breaths. Tears stared streaming down her face. She stepped aside to take a moment alone with Graccia's body. The forest stood silent, enfolding us in its magic. After a long pause, Chris politely pointed out the red-tailed hawk calls he detected moving through the canopy. We paused and heard faintly familiar voices. They were definitely the same phrase and tone as a red-tail, but there was something otherworldly about the way the voices traveled through the trees, and there were so many! Eva walked over and handed Graccia to me. I lifted her still body from the blanket and carefully laid the blanket across the base of the open grave. I leaned down and gently placed Graccia in the grave.

We stood over her body, taking our final looks at this life container for a gorgeous spirit. Her body looked small, no longer held large by such a strong presence. I picked up a small box and opened it. Inside I had one amethyst each for Graccia, Eva, and I, along with a string of red garnets for Graccia. I'd set aside two garnets from the string for Eva and myself. I handed Eva her amethyst stone and small red garnet. She took them into the palm of her hand. I reached down to place the amethyst for Graccia under her right wing while Eva placed the white mouse inside Graccia's talons. Next, I draped the strand of red garnets over Graccia's feet. "There's no place like home," I whispered. As I shifted her body around in the grave, the amethyst fell to rest at her crippled elbow, just where it needed to be. I picked up my drum and played my mallet against the hide for a time. While the beats carried through the lush forest I saw Graccia's spirit lift from her body and fly up to meet a whole kettle of hawks in the sky. Eva looked up and saw Graccia's spirit perched on a tree limb high above our heads. I rotated the open face of my drum towards Graccia's body and struck the hide hard to clear any remaining pieces of spirit left in the flesh. Then I softly brought the beats to a close.

Together we stood in circle and read the prayer for Graccia I had recited that morning. Eva and I knelt down at the grave and tucked the blanket around Graccia's body, saying goodbye with so many tears. Chris went to get the shovel and I pushed it out of the way. "Get that morbid thing out of here."

Passionately, I reached out and began moving the earth with my hands. The soft, moist hummus flowed like purifying water between my fingers and graced my senses with the smell of life. Eva and Chris joined me in filling the hole with handfuls of dirt. It felt good to make contact with the ground after so many hours of being apart from this world. Once the small hole was filled we delicately set to rearranging the mat of moss over the grave. All was as it should be. I stood back and carefully memorized the contour of this location before turning to leave.

We packed up and Chris pointed out the red-tail calls again. The cries were coming from all around us. He commented that it didn't quite sound like red-tails and was maybe starlings. I didn't think it was starlings, but agreed that it wasn't exactly red-tail voices either. Eva admitted that she liked to believe it was the voices of a dear friend mingled with her tribe. On our way out of the forest we passed Buckwheat and he stood up to join us on our walk back to the house.

We choose to hike up the steep "goat herder" trail to the house and a cacophony of sound erupted overhead. We looked up. It was an entire family of Stellar's jays fussing in a tall conifer. We recognized them instantly with their sleek, iridescent dark blue coats and black heads.

The mohawks on their crowns rose and fell and they cried at one another and danced among the branches.

"Maybe the hawk calls we heard were actually Stellar's jays imitating hawks," I wondered out loud. It was hard to believe as we watched them because they made harsh squawks at each another and clearly sounded like jays. My curiosity was unwavering. Eva didn't want me to ruin the thought of red-tails soaring over the canopy during Graccia's memorial ceremony, but against her wishes, I did some investigation. In the section on Stellar's jays in my bird song CD, the narrator had the following insight: "be especially careful for the Stellar's jay's imitation of a red-tailed hawk." This brought me the satisfaction of being right, but still left a mystery at hand. By some stroke of otherworldly guidance, these jays sensed the proper time to fill the forest with hawk cries. During all of our subsequent visits to the property, we never again heard an entire flock of jays use that cry. We never again witnessed a single jay call like a red-tail with that kind of intensity and persistence.

I've often wondered since that day about this profound connection between the hawks and the jays. The Stellar's jay and red-tailed hawk are not the only pairing of this kind. There are other species of jays that imitate other species of hawks. Much folklore relates the hawk as a messenger of the heavens, bringing the human race wisdom from the gods. To look at all the messages hawks carry from the heavens is to liken them to a cargo plane carrying crates of mail. However, human and hawk interactions in the wild are not always intimate, common, or prolonged. Hawks spend so much time in the air and the treetops that most people do not have the kind of direct interactions with them that I was the beneficiary of.

Jays, on the other hand, interact with people regularly. They frequent backyard bird feeders, accompany campsites, and often follow humans as they hike through the forest. In most neighborhoods, jays help compose of the symphony of bird song and the tapestry of bright plumage. They are the mail couriers that bring an envelope of insight to our boxes daily.

Eva and I sat on the back deck of the house in the crisp afternoon overlooking the orchard and forest beyond. Chris was inside cooking up a soothing garden vegetable soup for lunch. Buckwheat napped at our feet, his old joints soothed by the sun. We heard the Stellar's jays imitating the hawks on and off over the hours. The cries always came from the location of Graccia's grave. We'd look in the direction, look at each other, and smile. The company was reassuring.

The drive home was quieter than the drive out. We took the direct route and, each in our own mind, began to consider the coming days. The sun set behind us and before us the dusky sky changed shades. Dazed and exhausted, I didn't pay much attention to my surroundings. Luckily, we were headed due east.

We came into town, crested over a hill, and all at once lost our breath. There before us rose a plump harvest moon. She loomed over the landscape, seemingly four times as large as usual. We were fortunate not to drive off the road, transfixed by her splendor. I saw nothing but her. The majestic orb practically filled the span of the windshield. Her cheeks were tinted a lovely shade of peach that complemented the light sky she danced in. When I swore I'd never see the hawk covering the earth I had no idea the mythic bird would appear in this cosmic form. I wished I could reach the heavenly body during those few stellar moments when she was at the peak of her glory. I breathed a deep sigh of remorse when she quietly slipped higher into the heavens and shrank back to her ordinary brilliance. The stars had aligned and now the gate swiftly closed. The soothing rays of the lady harvest moon had offered my heart reassurance. I knew the gracious one and I would meet again.

Epilogue

When I journeyed to work out the ceremony for Graccia's burial I was shown three bridges, two arched and one flat. My spirit horse told me that the arched bridges symbolized deaths and the flat bridge symbolized a goodbye. I knew one of the arched bridges was for Graccia's passing and the flat bridge was for when I would have to leave my beloved companion, the horse named Caruso. At the time, I could not imagine or face who would be the second death.

Two months to the day after Graccia's death and burial, we had to put my eleven-year-old yellow lab, Buckwheat, to sleep. He passed at 9:17 a.m., and we quickly realized the synchronicity. Graccia was buried on September 17th (9/17). Buckwheat had taken desperately ill with little warning or explanation. In the end the vet guessed he'd had a brain stem tumor. We didn't think our hearts could ache any worse. Two months after Buckwheat's passing, Chris and I scattered his ashes into an estuary he had swum in with harbor seals. A few days after that, I had to say goodbye to Caruso and the herd of horses I'd come to love dearly.

We packed up our house into a moving truck, and loaded Gretchen into the back seat of our car. I was down to one extremely patient black cat. Despite the fact that we were driving halfway across the country in the dead of winter, we encountered little ice and snow. My parents took us in for a few months while we settled into new jobs. I continued on with my shamanic schooling and Chris and I started a new home. Thalia, Graccia, Buckwheat, and Caruso continued to assist my work in spirit, dreams, and journeys. I had a loving circle of classmates to share my learning experience with. My confidence grew.

A little over a year after our move to Colorado, I was offered a position living and working on a horse ranch. This had been a dream I'd formulated around the time I first met Thalia. The warm summer evening after we moved our two cats and belongings into the large ranch house, I set up my computer to check my email. There was a letter from my former boss at the fox captive breeding project. I hadn't talked to him in years. He was writing to report that all the foxes had finally been set free on the island. They were raising their pups in the wild now and thriving.

I sat soaking in the synchronicity of it all. How lovely. They were free and so was I.

I believe Thalia and Graccia came into my life for a reason. This story is it. Nothing that happened in their lives was a mistake. I truly understand how important this story is because they gave their lives to it. The maiden harrier and gracious red-tail were my best friends, my deepest confidants, my spirit mirrors. What a gift to look yourself in the face and love every breath, every mile, every day of what you see. What a gift.

Glossary of Terms

Bate When a bird jumps off her handler's glove because she is startled or nervous.

Helping spirit Spirits typically in human form that travel with and guide a shaman. They are able to travel to lower world and/or upper world. They can appear as ancestors, angels, archetypes, and more.

Jesses The soft leather straps that are placed around a raptor's ankles for use in falconry. These need to be oiled from time to time so they don't crack and break off.

Jess-up The act of hooking the leash to jesses before taking the raptor out of her cage.

Keel A bird's breastbone. It sticks out from the ribs. The amount of flesh along this bone indicates how skinny or overweight a bird is and, thus, what condition they are in.

Lower world A world that the shaman travels to. Reached by going through a hole in the ground, roots in a tree, cave, or body of water and passing through some sort of veil, membrane, or tunnel. Usually has natural landscapes and earthly features.

Mews   The name for a bird of prey enclosure or cage. The word "mews" came from French *muer*, "to change," because falconry birds were put in the mews while they were moulting or changing feathers.

Middle world   A world that the shaman travels to. The world we live in, but outside of time and space. Here a shaman can cover large distances and stretches of time in a matter of seconds.

Outback   The part of Willow Brook Wildlife Rehabilitation Center furthest from the clinic. There are no cages or buildings there and lots of open views.

Power animal   Animal spirits that travel with and guide a person on a shamanic journey. These can be real world animals such as a bear, fox, or hawk, or mythic animals such as a dragon, phoenix, or unicorn.

Rouse   When a bird raises all of her feathers and shakes from head to tail. This is considered a sure sign of comfort and relaxation.

Shamanic journey   Trance states that a shaman enters to travel into other worlds, speak with spirits, and bring back healing and guidance. In the modern day, shamanic practitioners typically enter trance states via rhythmic percussion.

Soul loss   When a part of a person's power/energy/soul is lost due to a traumatic event.

Soul part   Can be viewed as a piece of a person's power, energy, essence, or soul.

Soul retrieval   The process through which a shamanic practitioner journeys to another world to seek out, speak with, and bring back lost soul parts for a client.

Swivel　A piece of hardware commonly used to connect the jesses to the leash. The swivel allows the falconer to untwist a raptor's jesses without untwisting the length of the leash.

Upper world　A world that the shaman travels to. Reached by flying on the back of a power animal, riding a tornado or wind, or climbing a tree, mountain, or ladder, and passing through some sort of veil or membrane. Usually an ethereal environment unlike our own.

Resources

Andrews, Ted. *Animal Speak: The Spiritual and Magical Powers of Creatures Great and Small*. St. Paul, MN: Llewellyn Publications, 2003.

Brezsny, Rob. *Pronoia is the Antidote for Paranoia*. Berkley, CA: Frog, Ltd, 2005.

Eliade, Mircea. *Shamanism: Archaic Techniques of Ecstasy*. Trans. Willard Trask. London: Penguin Books, 1989.

Harner, Michael. *The Way of the Shaman*. New York: HarperCollins, 1990.

Ingerman, Sandra. *Medicine for the Earth: How to Transform Personal and Environmental Toxins*. New York: Three Rivers Press, 2000.

Ingerman, Sandra. *Soul Retrieval: Mending the Fragmented Self*. New York: HarperCollins, 1991.

Magee, Matthew. Peruvian Shamanism: The Pachakuti Mesa. Kearney, NE: Morris Publishing, 2005.

Myss, Caroline. *Sacred Contracts: Awakening Your Divine Potential*. New York: Harmony Books, 2001.

Palmer, Jessica. *Animal Wisdom: The Definitive Guide to the Myth, Folklore and Medicine Power of Animals*. London: HarperCollins, 2002.

Rain, Mary Summer and Alex Greystone. *Mary Summer's Guide to Dream Symbols*. Charlottesville, NC: Hampton Roads Publishing, 1996.

Sams, Jamie and David Carson. *Medicine Cards*. New York: St. Martin's Press, 1999.

Walsh, Roger. *The World of Shamanism: New Views on an Ancient Tradition*. Woodbury, MN: Llewellyn Publications, 2007.

Illustrations

The female northern harrier hawk that was my companion on
early morning walks on the island.

Four northern harrier nestlings hatched on the island and the
addled egg.

The last fledging flying from the nest below the runway on the island.

During one of our first visits together alone, Thalia with a full crop and a leg cocked, comfortable in her mews.

Thalia in the grass of her large outdoor mews.

Papa Rhett, the barn
owl, out in the yard
late one evening.

In her first week in captivity, this is Graccia in her immature plumage.

In full adult plumage, Graccia rests after her evening meal.

Graccia's ankles with leather jesses in her indoor mews.

Graccia, the angel of fiery red trees and golden grasses.

About the Author

 Stacey L. L. Couch describes herself as a shamanic cowgirl who works as a publicist and journalist for Mother Nature. A pioneer at heart, she empowers people with the ability to explore life's big questions. She aims to show how to form a real connection with our own souls through the natural world. A life-long student of nature, she has a biology degree in ecology and conservation as well as a 2-year shamanic certification. Her home on a 38-acre ranch is in Pagosa Springs, CO. She offers shamanic healing and teaching services at www.wildgratitude.com.